ANYWAY ANYTIME ANYWHERE

VOLUME II

TEXAS BAPTIST MEN MINISTRIES
THE STORY CONTINUES

KEN CAMP

Published February 2018 by Texas Baptist Men, Dallas, Texas.
ISBN-13: 978-0-692-05940-1

TABLE OF CONTENTS

PREFACE

Texas Baptist Men volunteers take to heart the admonition recorded in James 1:22: "Be doers of the word, and not merely hearers who deceive themselves" (NRSV). They understand "the word" commands them to love God and love other people. They are "doers" who recognize actions demonstrate love. They do not deceive themselves or anyone else. They are not fooling anybody. They are the real deal.

For 50 years, TBM volunteers have worked faithfully in churches to show boys in Royal Ambassadors what it means to be godly men. They have ministered in jails and prisons—both to incarcerated individuals and to often-underappreciated correctional officers. They have constructed churches and built finely crafted furniture for retreat centers, children's homes and other ministries. They have provided pure water in areas where it was lacking. They have served meals, cleaned homes, cleared debris and listened attentively to survivors of disasters throughout Texas and around the world.

This book seeks to tell their story. It is illustrative, not exhaustive. It picks up the story in midstream, where the earlier volume—*Anyway, Anytime, Anywhere: Thirty Years of Texas Baptist Men Ministries*—ended. It concludes in late 2016/early 2017, but keep in mind the book's subtitle: The Story Continues. Indeed, it does. After the period recorded here, TBM disaster relief volunteers responded to a series of tornadoes that struck East Texas in spring 2017. Then on Aug. 25, 2017, Hurricane Harvey made its initial landfall near Rockport as a Category 4 storm before beginning its slow and deadly crawl up the Texas Gulf Coast. It led to the largest deployment ever of TBM disaster relief volunteers. Since TBM assumed responsibility for disaster recovery and rebuilding less than one year before Harvey hit, the story of TBM involvement after Hurricane Harvey has yet to be completed.

Someday, a historian will write a comprehensive chronicle of TBM. This is not that serious academic treatise. It simply is an effort to bear witness of God's work among God's people called Texas Baptist Men during one narrow slice of time.

Because TBM volunteers and their leaders are "doers of the word," they often have been too busy "doing" ministry to stop and record what they have done. It has fallen to others to report on their work. I count it one of the great privileges of my life to have spent more than three decades reporting on TBM—first with the communications office of the Baptist General Convention of Texas and, for most of the period covered in this book, as managing editor of the *Baptist Standard.* So, this book relies heavily on the archived *Standard* articles. Unless otherwise noted, when cities or churches are mentioned without a state name, those cities and churches are located in Texas.

SEVERAL WORDS OF APPRECIATION ARE DUE:

- Thank you to the past and current TBM staff, particularly Don Gibson, who invited me to tackle this project, and Mickey Lenamon, who saw it through to completion. I was honored to be asked to write it, and it has been a labor of love.

- Thank you to individuals who took the time to be interviewed specifically for this book—Ron Chapman, John LaNoue, Bill Pigott, Gary Smith and Dick Talley, to name a few.

- Thank you to the many TBM volunteers over the last couple of decades who took time away while on a building project or disaster relief site to respond graciously and patiently to a reporter's intrusive questions.

- Thank you to Marv Knox, former editor of the *Baptist Standard*, who granted me total freedom to cover TBM ministries, without ever questioning the investment of time and resources.

- Thank you to John Hall, who led the BGCT news office several years and provided solid reporting during an important period in TBM's history.

- Thank you to Looie Biffar, who designed the cover and layout for the book.

- Thank you to George Henson, who proofread the manuscript, and to Alison Wingfield, who proofed the galleys. Everybody needs a good proofreader and editor. I am grateful. That being said, any mistakes that remain are mine alone.

Honesty compels me to acknowledge a few regrets. I wish I had been able to devote more time to tracking down information and interviewing other sources. My apologies particularly to Jim Furgerson, whom I should have interviewed. I simply never made the time to schedule a trip to South Texas. The book is poorer for that omission.

Another deep regret is that we did not initiate the project until after God called Leo Smith home. Leo's reflections and remembrances would have been invaluable. We'll have to wait until we join him to hear his stories. That should occupy a pretty good piece of eternity.

ANYWAY ANYTIME ANYWHERE

VOLUME II

CHAPTER ONE

TIME OF TRANSITION

CHAPTER ONE:
TIME OF TRANSITION

People who understand Texas Baptist Men recognize it as a movement of God—not just a denominational group, a nonprofit organization or humanitarian agency. Certainly, they see it as more than the brick-and-mortar building in east Dallas County that serves as its headquarters. Even so, a careful look at the facility at 5351 Catron Dr. reveals unexpected insights about TBM in the 21st century.

The main facility—the Robert E. Dixon Missions Equipping Center—bears the name of the man who led TBM through its first three decades and shaped its character. TBM constructed the 45,200-square-foot building in 2000 on land leased from Buckner Baptist Benevolences—now Buckner International—for 99 years at a $1 per year rate. Even a cursory glance inside reveals evidence of the multiple ministries TBM includes—memorabilia from Royal Ambassador events for boys, finely crafted furniture constructed by volunteer builders and shelves lined with discipleship curriculum focused on spiritual renewal.

Connected to the Dixon Center is the John LaNoue Disaster Relief Complex, a 15,000-square-foot expansion completed in 2010 that includes bays to house an extensive fleet of disaster relief vehicles—a field kitchen, mobile command post, childcare trailer and other specialty "rolling stock." TBM named the building for the man who built the first Southern Baptist disaster relief mobile unit and worked with TBM disaster relief missions ranging from Iran to Japan—as well as unprecedented famine relief work in North Korea.

Just to the north of the complex, across a small parking lot, the Bill Pigott Builders' Center approaches completion. The facility will provide a permanent workshop for volunteer builders and a secure place to store their tools, trailers and other equipment. It is named for the volunteer who began working with TBM Builders in the mid-1990s and became the group's leader a few years later.

So, the Texas Baptist Men headquarters includes three buildings. Two honor men who led TBM through its early, formative decades. One honors a man who led a key ministry into the new millennium. It speaks of the nature of TBM—grounded in the past, responding to needs in the present and keeping an eye open for new opportunities as God opens doors in the future.

At another level, it echoes challenges TBM faced in the last couple of decades. First, TBM tried to honor its founding generation while moving—

sometimes haltingly—into a new day with new leadership. Furthermore, the organization not only struggled to bridge generational divides and leadership transitions, but also wrestled with a changing denominational landscape. While the Dixon Center and LaNoue Complex are in the city of Dallas, the Pigott Center is erected just across the line in the city of Mesquite. It's one organizational headquarters built in two municipalities. It's two buildings organically connected, while one is detached. Just as the physical facility straddles a border, TBM likewise found itself in a similar situation. During a time of denominational division, TBM sought to remain closely affiliated with the established Baptist General Convention of Texas, while at the same time seeking to minister to men in churches affiliated with the Southern Baptists of Texas Convention.

Changes in leadership

In September 1998, Bob Dixon retired as TBM executive director. He had joined the staff of the Brotherhood Department of the BGCT State Missions Commission in 1966 as state director for Royal Ambassadors. Three years later, he succeeded the first TBM executive secretary-treasurer, "Wimpy" Smith. In the decades that followed, he led TBM to develop a disaster relief ministry that became the prototype followed across the Southern Baptist Convention. Likewise, he led in all the other groundbreaking ministries TBM developed, leaving an indelible imprint on the organization.

In 1998, the TBM board overwhelmingly elected Jim Furgerson to succeed Dixon as TBM executive director. Furgerson had served with distinction in Vietnam as a naval aviator with the U.S. Marine Corps, flying more than 500 combat missions. After he retired from the military as a lieutenant colonel, he served with South Texas Children's Home in Beeville as director of campus life. He also worked with the Missouri Baptist Children's Home, the SBC Brotherhood Commission and the SBC Foreign Mission Board as director of its volunteer in missions program.[1] Furgerson had a long and fruitful history with TBM, having helped to create the TBM Aviation Fellowship and working closely with its Upward Bound program for young men. The board recognized him as a man of unquestioned courage and Christian commitment.

Changes in the denominational landscape

From the day he accepted the post as TBM executive director, Furgerson faced major challenges. Throughout the 1980s and 1990s, much of the

---

1.   Ken Camp and Orville Scott, *Anyway, Anytime, Anywhere: Thirty Years of Texas Baptist Men Ministries* (Baptist General Convention of Texas: Dallas, Texas, 1999), pp. 220-221.

country knew Southern Baptists as "battling Baptists" whose annual meetings inevitably drove ever-deeper wedges between rival factions in the national body. For most of that time, Texas Baptists—including Texas Baptist Men—managed to work together at the state level. However, after trustees of Southwestern Baptist Theological Seminary in Fort Worth fired President Russell H. Dilday in 1994, the national fight hit close to home, and a growing number of Texas Baptists ceased to identify with the SBC. Dilday's dismissal triggered other events in BGCT life—a change in how the BGCT viewed the Cooperative Program unified budget, creation of a Theological Education Committee and formation of the Effectiveness/Efficiency Committee.[2] Southern Baptist loyalists in Texas who continued to support SBC leadership saw each of those actions as evidence the BGCT was moving away from SBC. So, in turn, they took action to distance themselves from the BGCT. On Nov. 20, 1997, immediately after the BGCT annual meeting in Austin, leaders of the group that became the Southern Baptists of Texas Convention announced their intention to pull away from the BGCT and form their own state convention.[3]

Since its beginning, TBM had been an affiliated organization of the BGCT. It received operating funds from the statewide portion of the Cooperative Program budget, and gifts to the Mary Hill Davis Offering for Texas Missions provided TBM with the money needed for various ministry projects. At the same time, TBM worked hand-in-glove with the SBC—first through its Foreign Mission Board, Home Mission Board and Brotherhood Commission; later through its International Mission Board and North American Mission Board. Furthermore, some lay leaders of TBM were members of churches that eventually affiliated with the SBTC, while others were members of churches loyal to the BGCT.

In March 2000, the TBM Executive Board voted to begin the process to establish TBM as a nonprofit corporation separate from the BGCT. The board unanimously approved articles of incorporation at the recommendation of its policy committee, and the governing document stipulated membership in TBM is comprised of "members of Baptist men's groups in Baptist churches affiliated with the Baptist General Convention of Texas." A letter from the policy committee explained: "Since so many of the disaster response agencies require the responding groups to be officially approved nongovernmental organizations, this incorporating of TBM is a necessary procedure" for TBM to minister nationally and internationally. Speaking

---

2. Harry Leon McBeth, *Texas Baptists: A Sesquicentennial History* (BaptistWay Press, Dallas, Texas, 1998), pp. 431-436.

3. *Ibid.*, p. 455.

in favor of the recommendation, Furgerson noted it would "enable Texas Baptist Men to meet human needs and offer a cup of water in Jesus' name." At the same time, Jerry Bob Taylor of Brownwood, chair of the policy committee, emphasized the action did not change TBM's "organizational, theological, fraternal or cooperative relationship" with the BGCT. "We want a good, harmonious working relationship with the BGCT," Taylor said.[4]

In the months that followed, however, SBTC Executive Director Jim Richards invited TBM—along with several other BGCT-affiliated educational and benevolent institutions—to establish a formal "fraternal relationship" with the new breakaway convention. The relationship agreement he proposed stated: "Funding from churches, special offerings and even the budget of the SBTC is possible for entities in a fraternal relationship. After January 1, 2002, no funds will be forwarded through the SBTC to entities that do not have a fraternal relationship or affiliation."[5] Addressing the TBM board Feb. 15-17, 2001, Furgerson made his views known: "We choose to be affiliated with the Baptist General Convention of Texas. Since 1968, we have operated on a handshake agreement with the BGCT, ... a gentleman's agreement that says we will serve all the men of Texas, period. I want to keep it that way."[6] The board's policy committee offered no recommendation regarding a fraternal relationship with SBTC, but it did recommend a series of bylaw amendments—including one to open TBM membership to men from non-BGCT affiliated churches. After discussing the proposal with board members, the policy committee agreed to offer revised amendments to the board at its October meeting. At the Oct. 29, 2001, meeting in Dallas, the board approved the proposed amendment expanding the TBM universe of membership, along with a resolution that stated: "Texas Baptist Men stands ready to assist any Baptist church in Texas to lead men into a love relationship with Jesus Christ which thrusts them and their families into a lifestyle of missions and ministry." At the same time, the board amended the constitution and bylaws to include a statement declaring TBM "an affiliate of the Baptist General Convention of Texas."[7]

The question of TBM's relationship to the BGCT remained a lively topic, however. In part, it grew out of recognition the international ministries of TBM had grown beyond the ability of the BGCT to fund the organizational

4. Ken Camp, "Texas Baptist Men headed toward incorporation," *Baptist Standard*, March 1, 2000, p. 9.

5. Ken Camp, "Texas Baptist Men loyal to BGCT; will continue to serve all churches," *Baptist Standard*, Feb. 26, 2001, p. 2.

6. *Ibid.*

7. Ken Camp, "Texas Baptist Men opens membership to non-BGCT churches," *Baptist Standard*, Nov. 5, 2001, p. 8.

fully. In May 2001, the TBM finance committee approved a $938,204 budget for the next year—about $300,000 more than the amount anticipated through the BGCT Cooperative Program. Like other entities that received Cooperative Program funds, the BGCT asked TBM to base its requests for the next year at 90 percent of the approved 2001 budget. However, TBM leaders wanted to respond to what they considered "invitations from God to join in his activity" around the world. So, the finance committee took "a step of faith," Furgerson said, and determined to appeal directly to the men of Texas to support TBM financially.[8]

Furthermore, SBTC leaders would not let the matter die, insisting that unless TBM recognized the group as a viable convention, there could not be any working relationship. Members of a TBM task force on convention relations who met with Richards became convinced unless TBM established a formal relationship with SBTC, the new convention would form its own competing men's organization within a matter of months. So, at a Feb. 15-16, 2002, board meeting at Latham Springs Baptist Encampment, a task force of former TBM presidents and retired staff presented a resolution expressing TBM's desire for a working relationship with the BGCT, SBTC, the Southern Baptist Convention and all associations of Texas Baptist churches. Dixon served a key role on that group, having been both the longtime executive director and the immediate past president, since he was elected to that post immediately after he retired. After extended discussion, the 197-member board voted 44-15 to approve the resolution as recommended. However, Leo Smith, a retired pastor from LaMarque who was elected TBM president the previous October, estimated at least 20 percent of the members present abstained from voting. Quoting from Henry Blackaby—co-author of *Experiencing God* and a guiding force in TBM spiritual renewal ministries—Smith noted when a vote by a body of Christians is not strong and not clearly decisive, the matter being considered is not in God's timing. So, citing "principles of spiritual leadership," he ruled the matter was tabled "until the Father himself takes it off."[9]

New leadership for a new day

In the months ahead, Smith had to step up to accept additional leadership responsibilities, after Furgerson left the executive director's position. When the TBM board named Smith to become interim executive director, he stepped down from the president's role and accepted the administrative

---

8. Ken Camp, "Texas Baptist Men take 'step of faith' with '02 budget," *Baptist Standard*, June 4, 2001, p. 3.

9. Ken Camp, "Texas Baptist Men board deliberates relationship to alternative convention," *Baptist Standard*, Feb. 25, 2002, pp. 3, 11.

responsibility. Smith had been involved with Royal Ambassadors since the mid-1960s, when the missions program for boys was coordinated by the BGCT Brotherhood Department. After TBM formed as a self-governing organization, Smith served in a variety of vice presidential roles and on multiple committees, before he became the first pastor elected as president of the laymen's missions organization. His congregational experience and pastoral temperament served him well as he guided TBM through delicate days, seeking to build bridges to enable TBM to continue to serve all the Baptist men of Texas.

For several months, Smith and other TBM leaders worked to craft a statement that would enable TBM to develop a working relationship with SBTC, without denying its historic connection to the BGCT or endangering that continuing partnership. At a Feb. 15 meeting at Latham Springs Baptist Encampment, the TBM Executive Board unanimously approved a resolution affirming TBM's "unique affiliation and partnership" with the BGCT but recognizing the SBTC and pledging to "officially work" with it in a "mutually supportive relationship." The resolution did not require any promise of financial support from SBTC. The resolution included a brief statement of faith, affirming TBM's belief in the Bible as a completely accurate final authority for faith and practice, salvation by grace through faith in Jesus Christ, Jesus as the model for ministry and a Christian calling to minister. It did not include the politically charged term "inerrancy" or make any reference to the controversial 2000 version of the Baptist Faith & Message. "This can be a resounding statement to all that we can dialogue and do kingdom work," Smith said.[10]

TBM Executive Director Leo Smith preaches to a Woman's Missionary Union of Texas rally.

So, TBM staked out a position between the two statewide Baptist conventions, seeking to minister to members of churches affiliated with the Baptist General Convention of Texas and the Southern Baptist Convention of Texas. In large part, it reflected TBM's desire to continue working with people who had been a vital part of the missions organization since its

---

10. John Hall, "Texas Baptist Men retains relation with BGCT, will work also with SBTC," *Baptist Standard*, Feb. 24, 2003, p. 2.

---

beginning. Historically, TBM had been strongest in the Dallas-Fort Worth area and East Texas—regions where SBTC first made inroads in recruiting churches. That meant lay leaders in those churches who were active in various TBM ministries found themselves members of churches that had become affiliated with SBTC. It also reflected the desire of TBM's elected leaders and staff to focus on ministry rather than denominational politics and to provide a place where all Texas Baptist laymen could serve the cause of Christ. "My hope is that Texas Baptist Men will be able to walk between the two conventions with integrity and a vision of bridging the gap for the laymen," Smith said.[11]

At its Feb. 26-28, 2004, meeting in Latham Springs Baptist Encampment, the TBM board of directors unanimously elected Smith as executive director—a post he had filled in an acting or interim capacity for nearly two years. "I am very humbled by your trust and want to pledge to you, and under God, that I will do all I can to hear his voice and lead Texas Baptist Men in a way that glorifies him," Smith told the board, adding he intended to "turn you loose to do what God has called you to do."[12]

After visiting a TBM Builders construction site, TBM Executive Director Leo Smith stops by to visit with the builders' wives as they work on crafts for a missions project.

Smith served as executive director more than seven years. When he assumed the post, the TBM annual budget was less than $1 million, and the BGCT Cooperative Program accounted for most of the funds. By the time he retired, he was administering $3.2 million annually, including designated disaster relief funds, and BGCT support leveled out at about $500,000 per year, not

11. Ken Camp, "Texas Baptist Men attempts to walk between two Texas Baptist bodies," Nov. 21, 2003, https://www.baptiststandard.com/resources/archives/43-2003-archives/1256-texas-baptist-men-attempts-to-walk-between-two-texas-baptist-bodies112403.

12. John Hall, "TBM names Smith executive director, agrees to work with SBTC on disaster relief ministry," March 5, 2004, https://www.baptiststandard.com/resources/archives/44-2004-archives/1639-tbm-names-smith-executive-director-agrees-to-work-with-sbtc-on-disaster-relief-ministry30804.

counting designated funds, projects funded through the Mary Hill Davis Offering for Texas Missions or gifts raised through the efforts of the Texas Baptist Missions Foundation. Although the BGCT no longer provided the bulk of TBM's annual budget, the state convention Cooperative Program remained the single largest source of funding, and Smith acknowledged TBM's close relationship with the BGCT. "We've tried to be a good partner with the BGCT, and the BGCT has been a good partner with us," he said. "It's not about money. It's about obedience. I've learned that when you obey, God provides."[13] Smith died April 28, 2013, after a battle with cancer.

Back to the future

When Smith retired in 2011, the TBM board looked to a longtime leader and staff member as interim leader—Don Gibson. About six months later, they elected Gibson, age 74, as the organization's fifth executive director. He brought to the position nearly 40 years experience with TBM. "I've tried to retire twice, but God had something else in mind," he said at the time.[14]

The TBM board elected Don Gibson as the missions organization's fifth executive director in 2011. He brought nearly 40 years experience with TBM to the role. After he retired in December 2015, Gibson continued to be involved in discipleship and restorative justice ministry, gathering Bibles and other Christian literature for prison chaplains.

In the 1970s, Gibson and his wife, Lena, initially became involved with TBM through lay renewal as members of Fellowship Baptist Church in Houston. In 1982, he felt God leading him to resign his position as an engineering manager in Houston. Gibson went to the TBM office in Dallas to visit with Executive Director Bob Dixon, and he took with him the prayer journal he used in his daily devotions. He showed Dixon multiple entries where he recorded his sense that God was leading him to resign his job to serve in lay ministries with TBM. Dixon responded by tell him he had been

---

13. Ken Camp, "Texas Baptist Men executive director announces retirement," *Baptist Standard*, Jan. 31, 2011, pp. 2, 18.

14. Ken Camp, "TBM names Gibson executive director," Nov. 6, 2011, https://www.baptiststandard.com/news/texas/13184-tbm-names-gibson-executive-director.

praying several years for someone to join the staff to work in lay ministries, but there was one problem—no money in the TBM for his salary. However, several laymen formed a nonprofit organization—Lay Renewal Ministries—and named Gibson its executive director. His job description had one line item: Follow God's direction. So for five years, Gibson served TBM as a Mission Service Corps volunteer, while Lay Renewal Ministries paid his salary. Eventually, his staff role as director of lay ministries was incorporated into the TBM budget. Serving in that capacity, he led TBM to expand its involvement in prison ministry, as it became a more fully rounded restorative justice ministry. He also piloted the first Experiencing God weekends, based on the discipleship study written by Henry Blackaby and Claude King. Gibson left the TBM staff to work directly with Henry Blackaby Ministries from 2002 to 2007, but he continued to work as a TBM volunteer. He returned to the TBM staff in 2008 as church renewal consultant and men's ministry coordinator. He served as executive director from 2011 until he finally succeeded in retiring Dec. 31, 2015.[15]

Leaders for a new millennium

When Gibson retired as TBM executive director, the organization's board of directors called on Mickey Lenamon to serve as interim leader. In less than five months, the board recognized they had found their sixth executive director, overwhelmingly electing Lenamon, age 58, to the post.[16]

Mickey Lenamon (left) was elected executive director of TBM in May 2016. Three months later, John Travis Smith (right) was named chief operating officer. They are pictured with Dani Clary, who volunteers her services as a pilot to help TBM.

Lenamon grew up in Travis Avenue Baptist Church in Fort Worth and had been involved with TBM since he was in elementary

15. Ken Camp, "Don Gibson to retire as Texas Baptist Men executive director," Dec. 3, 2015, https://www.baptiststandard.com/news/18562-gibson-to-retire-at-texas-baptist-men-executive-director.

16. Ken Camp, "Lenamon elected Texas Baptist Men executive director," May 11, 2016, https://www.baptiststandard.com/news/texas/19074-lenamon-elected-texas-baptist-men-executive-director.

school, accompanying his father, Joe T. Lenamon, to state Royal Ambassador events and various ministry projects. The elder Lenamon was elected a TBM vice president when the organization formed and served as president in 1974-77. When 8-year-old Mickey attended his first RA Camp at Latham Springs Baptist Encampment in 1966, he met Bob Dixon, who became a lifelong mentor. As a teenager, Mickey worked on the state RA staff, served with a church-starting mission effort in St. Cloud, Minn., and participated in lay renewal events throughout Texas, in five other states and in Australia.

Lenamon attended Texas A&M University and worked as a personal financial planner in Fort Worth before moving to Phoenix, Ariz., where he became a lay leader in North Phoenix Baptist Church. Later, he joined the staff of Baptist Senior Life Ministries in Phoenix as director of donor relations. In 1999, he returned home to work as vice-president of the Texas Baptist Missions Foundation. During his years with the foundation, he facilitated capital fund-raising campaigns for Baptist Student Ministries at Texas A&M University and Stephen F. Austin State University.

In 2006, Lenamon joined the TBM staff as director of resource development. Two years later, he was named associate executive director with specific responsibilities in donor relations. Working in that capacity, he directed a capital campaign to raise $1.2 million to build the John LaNoue Disaster Relief Complex, and he developed an annual giving program that raised more than $28 million for TBM in a decade. He also planned and led a dozen international mission trips.

When he accepted the executive director's role, Lenamon articulated several goals. He wanted to return TBM, which had grown increasingly dependent on paid staff, to its roots as a volunteer-led organization. He wanted to reach out to churches to engage them in TBM. He also wanted TBM to attract a rising generation of leaders. With the latter two goals in mind, he recommended to the board the hiring of John-Travis Smith, age 32, as chief operating officer.[17] Smith grew up in Royal Ambassadors, and he served TBM in multiple roles, including vice president for finance and a member of the TBM Forever Foundation board. As chief operating officer, Smith manages overall financial operations for TBM, oversees office staff and updates policies and procedures for accounting, human resources and other operations. Before he joined the TBM staff—first as interim chief operating officer in March 2016 and than in the permanent post five months later—Smith was pastor to young adults at First Baptist Church in Bryan. Previously, he served 11 years at First Baptist Church in Hempstead in

---

17. Ken Camp, "TBM names chief operating officer," Aug. 24, 2016, https://www. baptiststandard.com/news/texas/19430-tbm-names-chief-operating-officer.

various roles—youth minister, associate pastor and eventually interim pastor. Smith earned a bachelor of business administration degree in finance from Texas A&M and a master of divinity degree from Southwestern Baptist Theological Seminary.

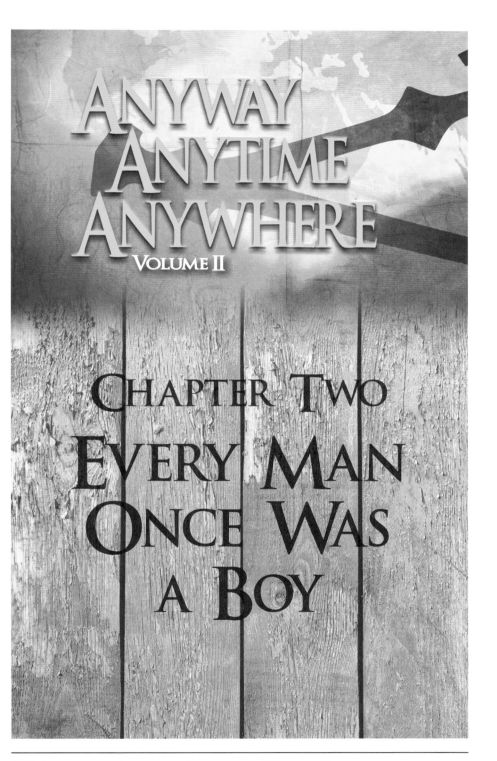

ANYWAY ANYTIME ANYWHERE

VOLUME II

CHAPTER TWO

EVERY MAN ONCE WAS A BOY

CHAPTER TWO:
EVERY MAN ONCE WAS A BOY

In a real sense, without Royal Ambassadors, Texas Baptist Men would not exist. Longtime Executive Director Bob Dixon first joined the Baptist General Convention of Texas Brotherhood Department staff in 1966 as state RA director. Likewise, John LaNoue, who

Royal Ambassadors enjoy spirited competition as they race handmade boats at an RA camp. (All RA photos courtesy of Keith Mack)

built the first disaster relief units and served as on-site coordinator for some of TBM's most memorable disaster relief deployments, began his work with TBM as state RA director. Leo Smith, who led TBM as executive director seven years, began his involvement with the group as an RA director. Mickey Lenamon, current TBM executive director, received his first introduction to the mission organization as a young RA and later as a state RA staff member. Royal Ambassadors served as the point of entry for many future TBM leaders.

Texas RAs entered the new century and new millennium under the leadership of Keith Mack, who became state RA and Challengers director in 1999. Mack became acquainted with RAs as a 10-year-old at Camp Copass, and it began his long-term commitment to the missions organization. As an adult, he served as RA counselor at Highland Village Baptist Church, RA director at First Baptist Church in Lewisville and Denton Baptist Association, and coordinator of RA Camp at Camp Copass.

In 2000, Texas RAs reported 1,156 chapters with a total enrollment of 19,850. That year, more than 1,600 attended the RA Congress in Belton, and 13 teams competed in the state basketball tournament. More than 5,000 boys attended RA summer camps, and 750 of the campers made spiritual decisions for Christ.[18] From 2000 to 2016, Mack reported 69,672 boys attended RA summer camps, resulting in 9,951 registered spiritual commitments.[19]

Accepting the Challenge

When the Pioneer Royal Ambassadors and the High School Baptist Young Men programs merged in 1994 to form Challengers for young men in grades seven through 12, leaders of the group in Texas took that name seriously. Four years after Challengers was launched, a half-dozen young men from Texas spent three weeks in Kenya, roofing five churches.[20] In the years that followed, Texas Challengers accepted increasingly more challenging mission projects.

Older Royal Ambassadors enjoy the challenge of a canoe trip.

In July 2000, eight Texas Baptist Challengers and four adult sponsors journeyed by boat more than 80 miles up the Rio Coco, separating Nicaragua and Honduras, to survey 30 Meskito Indian villages, as well as the Suma Indian village of Umbra.[21] The team served at the request of Jim and Viola Palmer, Southern Baptist missionaries to the Meskito Indians. The Texas Baptists traveled upriver in a 35-foot canoe-style boat with a 45 horsepower motor and in a small flat-bottom fiberglass motorboat, journeying about 20 miles a day. When the crew exhausted their initial 30-gallon supply of water, they spent hours purifying water and storing it in five-gallon bladders. In addition to seeking an accurate population count for the remote villages, the team sought to map the area, determine the physical needs of villagers and assess possibilities for long-range evangelism and church planting. They also

18. Keith Mack and Herb Weaver, *One Hundred Years of Royal Ambassadors* (Texas Baptist Men: Dallas, Texas, 2008), p. 154.

19. Email from Keith Mack, Oct. 31, 2016

20. Ken Camp and Orville Scott, *Anyway, Anytime, Thirty Years of Texas Baptist Men Ministries* (Baptist General Convention of Texas: Dallas, Texas, 1999), p. 27.

21. Ken Camp, "Texas teens survey Meskito Indian villages this summer," *Baptist Standard,* Sept. 11, 2000, p. 6.

showed the *"Jesus"* film depicting the life of Christ. The first three nights the team showed the film, it elicited little response. However, the fourth night, when the team showed it at the village of Santa Fe, 14 people made public faith commitments to Christ. The next month, during an evangelistic crusade in the region, four of the new believers paddled downriver more than four hours to attend the event and ask how a church could be started in their village.

In the years ahead, Challengers continued to serve around the world. Volunteers worked in Belize, Nicaragua, Kenya and the Ivory Coast in 2002.[22] In 2004, a Challengers team returned to Nicaragua to work with missionaries Jim and Viola Palmer at the Abundant Life Agricultural Center.[23] Additional missions opportunities followed

Royal Ambassador leaders teach boys lessons about responsibility and the importance of staying focused during time on an RA camp rifle range.

in succeeding years—sometimes in conjunction with younger Royal Ambassadors. For instance, Texas RAs and Challengers in 2007 collected money and purchased tools to send 190 filled toolboxes to Sudan in 2007 to help men there learn carpentry skills to support their families.[24] High school-aged young men also competed in the annual Challengers State Basketball Tournament and the missions Speak Out Tournament.

Marking a Century

Royal Ambassadors celebrated its centennial anniversary in 2008. To mark the occasion and record the mission organization's progress, Texas Baptist Men published a 158-page history, *One Hundred Years of Royal*

22. Ken Camp, "Texas Baptist Men board accepts missions opportunities," *Baptist Standard*, Feb. 25, 2002, p. 11.

23. 2004 *Texas Baptist Annual,* p. 168.

24. John Hall, "Texas Baptist Men send toolboxes to Sudan," June 22, 2007, https://www.baptiststandard.com/resources/archives/47-2007-archives/6641-texas-baptist-men-send-toolboxes-to-sudan.

Ambassadors, written by Keith Mack and Herb Weaver. Through decades of service, Weaver had been RA director at 7th & James Baptist Church in Waco, Gaston Avenue Baptist Church in Dallas, Lucas Baptist Church, North Dallas Baptist Church and Park Cities Baptist Church, as well as an RA leader both in Dallas Baptist Association and Union Baptist Association. He directed the Leadership Training Camp two decades and worked as state staff trainer. In their book, Mack and Weaver presented an overview of the resources used in RAs over the course of 100 years—curriculum, patches, pins and uniforms. Moreover, they presented a tribute to the leaders who made RAs possible and a testimonial to the organization's continued relevance. They wrote: "Committed leaders are the heart of the Royal Ambassadors

Whether eating hot dogs outdoors or learning crafts activities, Royal Ambassadors appreciate the meaningful time dedicated leaders spend with them.

program. Mission-minded Christian men serve as a living library of knowledge and provide a role model for boys to see what it means to grow in relationship with Christ. … RAs is the only program that is offered by Southern Baptists that encourages men to mentor boys and shows them how to become a man of God."[25]

Prior to the Baptist General Convention of Texas 2008 annual meeting in Fort Worth, TBM and Woman's Missionary Union of Texas met together to celebrate the RA centennial. RAs began as a WMU program and continued under WMU direction at the national level until the Southern Baptist Convention transferred the responsibility to the Brotherhood Commission in 1970. WMU gave birth to the program because its members saw the need for missions education for boys, Texas WMU Interim Director Nelda Seal told

25. Mack and Weaver, p. 126.

the assembly in Forth Worth. "We reluctantly turned them over because we felt they needed the leadership of men in the churches," Seal said.[26] Keith Mack told the crowd three things about RAs had not changed in 100 years—the motto, based on 2 Corinthians 5:20; the needs of boys; and the need for men to lead boys into a relationship with God in Christ. Other speakers included TBM Executive Director Emeritus Bob Dixon, Executive Director Leo Smith, former Texas WMU Executive Director-Treasurer Joy Fenner and BGCT Executive Director Randel Everett.

Royal Ambassador campcraft instructors use every opportunity to teach spiritual lessons.

When the Southern Baptist Convention approved a massive reorganization of its agencies in the 1990s, the Brotherhood Commission ceased to exist. Most of its ministries were divided between the new North American Mission Board and the Baptist Sunday School Board, which became LifeWay Christian Resources. NAMB received the assignment of missions education, including RAs and Challengers. While working with NAMB, Texas Baptist Men also provided additional Texas-specific resources and material for Texas RA leaders. From 2000 to 2005, TBM provided a series of planbooks that offered information about regional and state events and missions offerings, as well as information about how to launch new RA programs. TBM distributed the books free of charge to registered RA chapters and to associational trainers.[27] In 2007, TBM published *Campcraft—Outdoor Living Skills* as a manual for

26. "Combined TBM, WMU rally celebrates 100 years of missions education for boys," Nov. 10, 2008, https://www.baptiststandard.com/news/texas/8807-combined-tbm-wmu-rally-celebrates-100-years-of-missions-education-for-boys.

27. Mack and Weaver, p. 120.

RA and Challenger leaders, with a special focus on spiritual applications for outdoor activities.[28] In 2011, national Woman's Missionary Union announced it would reassume responsibility for producing resources for the RA program by fall of the next year.[29] Five years later, a young man with Texas Baptist ties joined the national WMU staff as a ministry consultant for RAs and Challengers—Zachariah Seanor, a graduate of Baylor University's Truett Theological Seminary and former minister to students at Taylor's Valley Baptist Church in Temple.[30]

Planting seeds, investing in lives

At weekly meetings in local churches, summer camps or statewide events such as RA Congress, RA Rally or Missions Mania, Royal Ambassador leaders use fun activities to attract boys and engage them in activities with Christian men who can teach them about Jesus. "I don't know if making a racecar ever saved a boy, but it can get them to a place where they hear the message of salvation," said Murrie Wainscott, a member of Central Baptist Church in Italy, who has worked with RAs for a quarter-century. "A lot of the boys we see are not church members. This may be their only opportunity to hear about the Lord and hear the plan of salvation. We may not see a lot of fruit right away, but we are planting seeds. It may be 20 years later when they have a family of their own that they see the need for the Lord in their lives."[31]

Sometimes, RA leaders use hands-on missions activities to engage boys. In 2011, RA chapters around the state built bookcases and purchased children's Bibles and other books for impoverished children living in colonias along the Rio Grande. RAs brought the bookcases and home libraries to Missions Mania at Latham Springs Baptist Encampment, where they were presented to Literacy Connexus as part of the Books for the Border project. Boys enjoyed working with power screwdrivers and other tools; leaders took advantage of the opportunity to talk with them about helping other children learn about Jesus. "The value of godly men teaching boys how to use tools and having an impact on their lives never goes out of style," Wainscott said.[32]

---

28. *Ibid.*, p. 119.

29. Ken Camp, "WMU to produce RA materials," May 18, 2011, https://www.baptiststandard.com/news/baptist/12528-wmu-to-produce-ra-materials.

30. Julie Walters, "Texas Baptist named national WMU ministry consultant for boys," July 26, 2016, https://www.baptiststandard.com/news/baptist/19328-texas-baptist-named-national-wmu-ministry-consultant-for-boys.

31. Ken Camp, "Taking fun and games seriously," *CommonCall*, May 2015, p. 12.

32. George Henson, "RAs at Italy church combat illiteracy along the Rio Grande," Nov. 3, 2011, https://www.baptiststandard.com/news/texas/13181-ras-at-italy-church-help-combat-illiteracy-along-rio-grande.

RA leaders always look for teachable moments when they can use common objects and activities to impart spiritual lessons. "We can be tying knots in a rope. It's a chance to talk about how life can be a tangled mess, and when it is, God can't use you to the fullest. We need to be coiled and ready for the Master's use," said Steve Darilek, RA director at Pleasant Valley Baptist Church in Bridgeport, who has worked with RAs since 1978.[33]

What RA leaders say to each boy matters, but many of the leaders agree they make the greatest impact simply by investing time, energy and attention in young lives. "Many don't have a father figure at home. They know there are men there (at RAs) who want to be with them," said Brad Blanchard, a veteran RA leader from Meadowbrook Baptist Church in Waco, where about one-third of the boys in RAs are from families who do not attend the church.

To illustrate that point, Steve Darilek pointed to an instance when the Dallas Cowboys were playing in the Super Bowl, and the game conflicted with the regularly scheduled RA meeting at Pleasant View Baptist Church. He told the boys if they attended the RA meeting that Sunday, he would teach them how to start a fire without using matches. "Not a one of them stayed home to watch the Cowboys," he recalled. However, he insists the boys were not drawn to the meeting by curiosity about fire-starting techniques. They attended because they realized men at the church cared more about them than about watching a football game. "The Dallas Cowboys weren't the ones investing in their lives. ... A lot of grown men have come back to thank me for investing in them," he said. "It's not about me. It's God making a difference in their lives through me."[34]

---

33. Camp, "Taking fun and games seriously," p. 14.
34. *Ibid.*

CHAPTER THREE
STILL BUILDING
FOR THE
GLORY OF GOD

CHAPTER THREE:
STILL BUILDING FOR THE GLORY OF GOD

Bill Pigott, state director of TBM Builders, worked on a project at Lake Athens Baptist Church in 2011 after the church's previous structure was destroyed by arson.

When Bill Pigott retired as a maintenance superintendent with the U.S. Air Force Reserve and as an inspector at Bell Helicopter in the mid-1990s, he sought a place to serve God. He found it with the Texas Baptist Men Builders. He helped build churches and work on construction projects at Baptist encampments. He spent an extended time on a building project at Breckenridge Village near Tyler, a residential community for mentally challenged adults developed by Baptist Child and Family Services. Before long, his hard work and leadership abilities caught the notice of Jim Furgerson, TBM executive director. Twice—at Riverbend Retreat Center and at a church-building project in Tahoe City, Calif.—Furgerson asked him to consider becoming special-projects coordinator for the builders. Twice, Pigott told him he just didn't feel right about it. Finally, Furgerson approached him a third time at Texas Baptist Encampment at Palacios. Furgerson told Pigott he felt God's leading to establish a volunteer director's position for the TBM Builders, and he was convinced Pigott was the man for the job. Reluctant to close a door of service God might be opening, Pigott conditionally agreed to accept the post for one year. The next year, newly elected TBM Executive Director Leo Smith asked Pigott to continue serving—and nobody ever asked him to stop.[35]

---

35. Interview with Bill Pigott at the Dixon Missions Equipping Center in Dallas, July 6, 2015.

Long-term project in Lubbock

Steve Jackson (standing) from Calvary Baptist Church in Midlothian and Charles Tompkins (kneeling) from First Baptist Church in Hallettsville work on framing a room inside Lake Athens Baptist Church.

In 2003, the TBM Builders tackled a major project on the South Plains. Shirley Madden had founded My Father's House as a ministry to low-income women. The ministry offered Christian Women's Job Corps training at Iglesia Bautista Templo in Lubbock, teaching job skills and life skills in a Christian context to unemployed or underemployed women. But Madden had a larger vision. She wanted to develop a residential program at a Living and Learning Center on 4.29 donated acres. She envisioned a center with 18 two-bedroom apartments, classrooms, a commercial kitchen, day care facilities and a laundry. She secured a $250,000 grant from the Meadows Foundation toward the project, along with a $150,000 no-interest loan from another Texas-based foundation. However, the project demanded extensive labor, and TBM Builders provided the bulk of it.[36]

Working in temperatures that plummeted from 103 to 48 degrees in less than 48 hours, the TBM Builders served in challenging circumstances. Builders accustomed to working with wood had to learn construction techniques using a heavy, load-bearing steel framework. For three months, the builders turned the Lubbock Independent School District's Lowrey Field into a mobile home community and its field house into a sewing factory where builders' wives worked on a variety of projects, including curtains and valances for the windows at the Living and Learning Center. Meanwhile, the TBM furniture

---

36. Ken Camp, "Builders make Lubbock home for three-month project," Oct. 10, 2003, https://www.baptiststandard.com/resources/archives/43-2003-archives/270-builders-make-lubbock-home-for-three-month-project60203.

builders transformed a motorboat showroom into a furniture mill, crafting beds, chests and tables for the center's apartments.

When the TBM Builders eventually left after three months, students in the Lubbock ISD's building trades classes went to work. Other volunteer builders also worked to complete the project.[37] For several years, My Father's House-Lubbock operated as an independent ministry, providing what Madden called "a second-chance place" for young women who often found themselves in desperate circumstances.[38] In 2008, My Father's House-Lubbock became part of Buckner Children & Family Services.[39] Seven years later, My Father's House-Lubbock joined Buckner Family Place ministries at several locations around the state under the Buckner Family Pathways umbrella.[40]

Bill Campbell, a longtime volunteer with TBM Builders, operates a saw on the construction site at his home church, Lake Athens Baptist.

Providing a place to worship

In some instances, churches that have met previously in homes, schools or storefronts gain a home of their own thanks to the TBM Builders. Pastor Monte Byrd launched Mill Creek Baptist Church of Bellville in his home. Later, worshippers met in a variety of venues—a community center, a school and even a German dance hall. After 10 years moving from one place to another, the TBM Builders

37. "Volunteers needed in Lubbock," Sept. 19, 2003, https://www.baptiststandard.com/resources/archives/43-2003-archives/886-lubbock92203.

38. Ken Camp, "My Father's House offers a safe home for a fresh start," July 21, 2006, https://www.baptiststandard.com/resources/archives/46-2006-archives/5292-my-fathers-house-offers-a-safe-home-for-a-fresh-start.

39. "Texas Tidbits," Feb. 29, 2008, https://www.baptiststandard.com/resources/archives/48-2008-archives/7615-texas-tidbits611.

40. Chelsea Q. White, "Buckner Family Place, My Father's House Lubbock become Buckner Family Pathways," Sept. 29, 2015, http://www.buckner.org/blog/buckner-family-place-my-fathers-house-lubbock-become-buckner-family-pathways/.

constructed a picturesque facility in 2007. Modeled after a church building Byrd saw in Brenham, the little church with the towering steeple sits atop

Grace Conner from First Baptist Church in Elgin works on a craft project to benefit children in Mexico. While the TBM Builders worked on rebuilding Lake Athens Baptist Church after it was destroyed by arson, their wives led a morning Bible study each morning open to anyone in the community, and they spent their afternoons working on craft projects.

a hill overlooking a major thoroughfare. "We're going from where nobody knows where we're at, to having one of the most visible spots in town," Byrd told a reporter when the builders were hard at work.[41] When the tall steeple arrived, Byrd learned a crane would be required to lift it into position, and the church had no money budgeted to rent one. However, the church's heating and air conditioning contractor learned about the need and offered to take care of it. "That's the way it's been throughout the whole project," Byrd said. "God's fingerprints are just everywhere. One thing after another, God has just taken care of it."[42]

Sometimes, TBM Builders literally have helped churches rise from the ashes. In 2010, Lake Athens Baptist Church near Athens lost its building to arson. "I'll never forget that night," Pastor John Green said months after the fire. "There were eight fire departments working on it. One truck had a spotlight on the church, shining on the steeple. Sometimes, it was almost blocked out by the smoke, but it always came back into sight. I knew

---

41. George Henson, "After 10 years, church finally has a home of its own," Feb. 2, 2007, https://www.baptiststandard.com/resources/archives/47-2007-archives/6110-after-10-years-church-finally-has-a-home-of-its-own .

42. *Ibid.*

our church would come back."[43] Indeed, the church's comeback began in January 2011 when 32 recreational vehicles rolled into the church's parking lot and the occupants of those vehicles started work rebuilding the facility. The TBM Builders helped the church construct a 16,000-square-foot building for the cost of a 10,500-square-foot building, noted R.B. Richardson, a charter member of the congregation.[44]

Meeting needs where they find them

The TBM Builders specialize in construction of church buildings and facilities for encampments, not homebuilding. However, the volunteers are open to opportunities as God presents them and eager to respond to needs as they discover them. For instance, after a tornado destroyed the tiny West Texas town of Saragosa on Memorial Day weekend in 1987, the TBM Builders took the lead on Labor Day weekend in rebuilding the community—a project that involved 700 volunteers.[45] So, when the TBM Builders helped two families in Cross Plains rebuild their homes in 2006, the project may have been a bit unusual but hardly unprecedented. A wildfire had affected more than 90 homes in the community and killed two people. City officials and leaders of First Baptist Church in Cross Plains identified two families the TBM Builders could assist. The TBM volunteers finished one home and rebuilt another in three weeks.[46]

On another occasion, the Hispanic TBM Builders worked on a small-scale project that made a big difference in the life of one little girl. A grandmother contacted TBM to ask whether volunteers could build a ramp so her 6-year-old granddaughter, Laurel Escochea, could enter and exit her Seagoville home without having to rely on others for assistance. Laurel was born with one leg shorter than the other. After beginning a series of corrective surgeries, she was able to use a walker on a limited basis but still needed a wheelchair for extended distances. Mike Tello of Weslaco knew the men at Primera Iglesia Bautista in Jacksonville already had experience on one home

---

43. Ken Camp, "Tireless retirees help burned-out church rise from the ashes," *Baptist Standard,* Jan. 31, 2011, p. 9.

44. *Ibid.*

45. Ken Camp and Orville Scott, *Anyway, Anytime, Anywhere: Thirty Years of Texas Baptist Men Ministries,* (Baptist General Convention of Texas: Dallas, Texas, 1999), pp.140-150.

46. John Hall, "TBM volunteers rebuild homes in Cross Plains," May 26, 2006, https://www.baptiststandard.com/resources/archives/46-2006-archives/5078-tbm-volunteers-rebuild-homes-in-cross-plains.

improvement project. So, he told the crew about Laurel's need, and they responded, constructing a ramp for the Escochea's home.[47]

In 2014, the TBM Builders returned to the Hospitality House in Huntsville—a ministry that provides lodging and meals for visiting families of inmates—to construct a children's activity building. Twenty-eight years earlier, TBM Builders led about 270 volunteers in an around-the-clock marathon project to construct the ministry's original facility. As the ministry grew, art therapy became an important tool to help the children of inmates express their feelings, and the activity building offered a safe and comfortable place for that activity. Art therapy proved "very successful with the children in giving them an outlet to talk about their frustrations," said Debra McCammon, who became executive director of the Hospitality House in 2009. "A lot of them are very bitter against their dads for committing crimes and for what it puts the family through."[48] The TBM volunteers worked alongside contractor Dan Phillips and his crew from Phoenix Commotion, a building initiative that uses recycled and salvageable materials in construction. Church groups and other volunteers provided much of the labor to complete finishing work on the facility.

A passion for excellence

Jack Tennison, a retired college math professor, and Eugene Esters, who worked for an aeronautics company, launched the furniture builders as a distinctive ministry within the larger TBM Builders in the late 1990s. After working together on other projects, the pair launched the specialized ministry by building furniture for apartments of needy families at the request of CityChurch in Amarillo. The ministry had received an estimate of $98,000 to equip 34 apartments with five pieces of furniture each, but Tennison expressed confidence the TBM furniture builders could do the job for $25,000 or less, including the purchase of tools. They completed the project for $18,000. In the process, they built a deep and abiding relationship with High Plains Christian Ministries Foundation in Amarillo, which provided the furniture builders with a tool trailer and also offered other support.

In their first 14 years, the furniture builders crafted more than 6,000 pieces of furniture to equip 17 camps in Texas—as well as Glorieta Baptist Conference Center in New Mexico, Canadian Southern Baptist Seminary

---

47. George Henson, "Hispanic builders make mobility easier for disabled 6-year-old girl," Nov. 5, 2012, https://www.baptiststandard.com/news/texas/14492-hispanic-builders-make-mobility-easier-for-disabled-6-year-old-girl.

48. Tyler Agnew, "Hospitality House adds getaway for young visitors," Aug. 19, 2014, https://www.baptiststandard.com/news/texas/16854-hospitality-house-adds-getaway-for-young-visitors.

Craftsmen Jack Tennison and Eugene Esters work together to build furniture for Baptist camps, children's homes, churches and other ministries. (Photo / David Clanton)

in Alberta, the Dixon Missions Equipping Center in Dallas and many churches and children's homes. In 2015, TBM's furniture builders and cabinet builders teamed up to produce more than 100 pieces of furniture for the women-in-crisis shelter operated by CareNet Pregnancy Center of Central Texas, along with cabinets for the guesthouse bedrooms and other facilities. While the men worked in a woodworking shop set up in an industrial park, their wives crafted quilts, baby blankets and bibs for CareNet. "It's our contribution to saving babies and maybe making future disciples," said project coordinator Harold Cheatham of Stephenville. "You never know what a child will become."[49]

Camp managers counted the furniture builders as some of their best friends and most valued supporters. "They have saved us a ton of money on some high-quality furniture. And any money we save, we can put into camping, which is our mission," said Mike Wilson, administrator at Alto Frio Baptist Encampment near Leakey. "More than that, they have become like another set of parents to us. They're like family."[50]

Along the way, the furniture builders developed a reputation as craftsmen with a passion for excellence. Most TBM Builders use tape measures before sawing; the furniture builders use calipers and micrometers. For years, Esters insisted on drawing precise building plans on his computer for every project. "Eugene is a perfectionist, and Jack is pretty close to it but won't admit it," said Buddy Nafe, who became coordinator for the TBM furniture builders in 2006 when Tennison stepped down from the role. "A drawer made

49. Ken Camp, "Building Peace of Mind," *CommonCall*, December 2015, p. 16.
50. Ken Camp, "Serving the Master Carpenter," *CommonCall*, March 2013, p. 7.

for Glorieta is interchangeable with the drawer of a chest at Piney Woods Encampment."[51]

A building for the builders

For most of their 37 years, the TBM Builders operated without a place they could call their own. They set up workshops on site at the churches, camps and other locations where they ministered. Tool trailers typically were housed at the Dixon Missions Equipping Center, along with the fleet of disaster relief equipment. However, if the tool trailers had to be parked outside the building, they became targets for thieves and vandals. Furthermore, some building projects demanded a workshop where volunteers could come and go as time permitted. So, at their fall 2013 meeting, members of the TBM Executive Board unanimously approved a proposal to construct an 8,000-square-foot building specifically for the TBM Builders on property adjacent to the Dixon Center.[52] TBM broke ground for the facility the following February, and in spite of his objections, the group agreed to name it in honor of Bill Pigott.

The project met unexpected hurdles. While the Dixon Center is built on property in the Dallas city limits, the builders' facility was planned on property just across the line in the Mesquite city limits. Building permits proved problematic. Furthermore, the cost of building materials escalated. Finally, 14 months after the ceremonial groundbreaking, TBM began work in earnest on the building as heavy machinery started preparing the ground for construction.[53] By mid-2016, the building was "in the dry," and volunteers started working on installing insulation and drywall. Volunteers continued working throughout the fall. At that point, TBM still was seeking additional funding to install the building's security system, phones, fire alarms and Internet.

From the group's earliest days, TBM Builders have met a vital need— providing free labor to allow congregations to build the facilities they needed to reach their communities for Christ and make disciples. Countless churches throughout Texas, particularly in rural areas, gather each week for worship in sanctuaries and assemble for Bible study in classrooms constructed by the TBM Builders. Between 2000 and 2016, the group worked on about 300 churches, not to mention the dozens of jobs crews worked on for Baptist

---

51. *Ibid.*, p. 8.
52. Stephanie Midkiff, "TBM board approves building for builders," Oct. 29, 2013, https://www.baptiststandard.com/news/texas/15722-tbm-board-approves-building-for-builders.
53. Grace Gaddy, "TBM begins work on 8,000-square-foot facility for builders," April 15, 2015, https://www.baptiststandard.com/news/texas/17692-tbm-begins-work-on-8-000-square-foot-facility-for-builders.

encampments every year, along with special projects such as visitation centers and chapels for Texas prisons. Overall, the TBM Builders typically complete anywhere from 45 to 60 projects a year. Specialized crews built finely crafted furniture and cabinets, and masonry crews laid bricks. In some instances, husband-and-wife teams work side-by-side in construction. More often, while the men are sawing, hammering and nailing, their wives typically hold Bible studies open to other people in the community and work on craft projects, typically donated to nursing homes or child-care facilities. Wherever they serve, the volunteers seek to share the love of God through word and deed. "If we build a building and don't have an impact on the community, we are wasting our time," Pigott said. "Our calling is not to build. It is to be a witness."[54]

---

54. Interview with Bill Pigott at the Dixon Missions Equipping Center in Dallas, July 6, 2015.

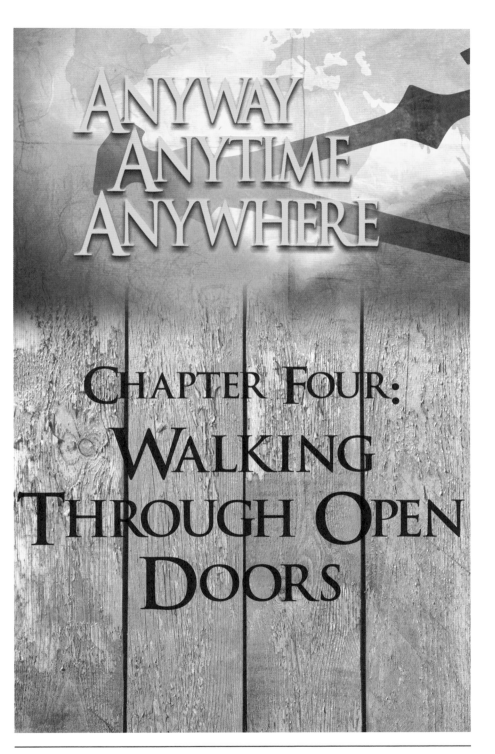

ANYWAY ANYTIME ANYWHERE

CHAPTER FOUR:

WALKING THROUGH OPEN DOORS

CHAPTER FOUR:
WALKING THROUGH OPEN DOORS

Thirty years ago, a director of missions from far-off Vancouver, British Columbia, revolutionized Texas Baptist Men and its approach to ministry. Henry Blackaby spoke to the 1987 TBM Convention in Fort Worth, describing principles he and Claude King soon would write about in an interactive workbook published by the Baptist Sunday School Board, *Experiencing God: Knowing and Doing the Will of God.*[55] Speaking to the TBM annual meeting, Blackaby presented what he grew to identify as the "seven realities" of Experiencing God: (1) God is always at work around you; (2) God pursues a continuing love relationship with you that is real and personal; (3) God invites you to become involved with him in his work; (4) God speaks by the Holy Spirit through the Bible, prayer, circumstances and the church to reveal himself, his purposes and his ways; (5) God's invitation for you to work with him always leads you to a crisis of belief that requires faith and action; (6) You must make major adjustments in your life to join God in what he is doing; and (7) You come to know God by experience as you obey him and he accomplishes his work through you.[56] Those principles transformed TBM from a program-driven denominational entity to a dynamic missions movement. "When we began looking at where God was working and responding to his invitations, we didn't have to drum up things to do," said Bob Dixon, who led TBM as executive director nearly three decades. "The Father kept giving us assignments. And when we were faithful, he would give us another one." [57]

The change in philosophy not only affected the organization, but also made a life-altering impact on its members who took to heart the principles of *Experiencing God.* Of course, TBM continued to involve members effectively in discipleship events and programs—established ones such as *Experiencing God* and *Fresh Encounter*, as well as new ones such as *No Man Left Behind.* However, over the last decade and a half, TBM's discipleship ministry could be measured less by the number of couples who participated in spiritual renewal weekends or the number of churches that sponsored the

---

55. Ken Camp and Orville Scott, *Anyway, Anytime, Anywhere: Thirty Years of Texas Baptist Men Ministries* (Baptist General Convention of Texas: Dallas, Texas, 1999), pp. 35-36.

56. Henry T. Blackaby and Claude V. King, *Experiencing God* (Broadman & Holman Publishing: Nashville, Tenn., 1998), pp. 49-64.

57. Ken Camp, "Experiencing God transformed TBM over last two decades," July 8, 2010, https://www.baptiststandard.com/news/texas/11357-experiencing-god-transformed-tbm-over-last-two-decades.

events and more by the number of ministries birthed out of what they taught and learned there.

For example, Fred and Evelyn Johnson initially became involved in lay renewal through a weekend event a TBM team led at First Baptist Church in George West more than 40 years ago. "We made the commitment to serve God wherever he wanted us to go, and God opened doors of opportunity," Evelyn Johnson said. "We promised we would go any way, any time, anywhere he called, and we've been from one end of the world to another."[58] For the Johnsons, that meant leaving their 857-acre South Texas cattle ranch and journeying to China twice to participate in prayer-walks, building homes in Honduras after a natural disaster and ministering in prisons in Ukraine, as well as participating in lay renewal events in Belize, Germany, Australia, the Netherlands, South Africa, Canada and Spain. Much closer to home, it meant leaving the comfortable surroundings of a church they loved to help launch a cowboy church.

"We were perfectly satisfied at church," said Fred Johnson, who had been part of First Baptist Church in George West more than four decades, serving as a deacon and Royal Ambassadors leader. "But when God spoke, it was time to go. ... It was like the Holy Spirit was tapping us on the shoulder."[59] After hearing a representative from the Texas Fellowship of Cowboy Churches tell a TBM meeting how God was using western-heritage churches to reach unchurched people, the Johnsons prayed about becoming involved. They joined a core group of 10 people from their congregation to start Brush Country Cowboy Church. For an extended period, the church event met at the Johnsons' ranch before the congregation moved to its own facility near Interstate 37.

"The type of people this church is reaching aren't going to go to any other church," Evelyn Johnson said. "We have people who have been working cattle come on to church with their spurs on. We have people working on farms who turn off the tractor and come on to worship. We have oil and gas workers—mechanics who are on call Sunday morning—who come to church in greasy overalls. Nobody thinks anything about it."[60] Furthermore, the Johnsons have led small-group studies of Experiencing God, introducing members of the nontraditional church to its principles.

Another example of TBM responding in obedience to a door God opened came in 2014 when the group's Military Fellowship responded to a plea

---

58. Ken Camp, "Accepting God's invitations wherever they lead," *CommonCall*, April 2013, p. 7.

59. *Ibid.*

60. *Ibid.*, p. 8.

for help from the organizers of a holiday party for military personnel and their families. The caterer who was supposed to prepare a Christmas meal for about 200 soldiers with the 354th Medical Company from Seagoville—many of them due to deploy to Afghanistan—and their families cancelled at the last minute. Representatives from the U.S. Army 341st Multifunctional Medical Battalion saw a disaster in the making. So, naturally, they called TBM for help. George Felkner, a layman at Mimosa Lane Baptist Church in Mesquite, fielded the call, and he rounded up seven other TBM volunteers—including four U.S. Navy veterans from the Vietnam conflict—to prepare and serve food. "Being veterans and dealing with all the stuff we did when we returned from Vietnam, we didn't want anybody else in the military to feel unappreciated," Felkner said, noting nobody—volunteers, soldiers or family members—felt any lack of appreciation at the event. "We walked in, and everybody started applauding." [61]

That event led to future opportunities. In September 2014, 16 TBM volunteers provided hamburgers and hot dogs for about 400 people at a "family day" picnic for the U.S. Army's 94th Combat Support Hospital Bravo Company in Seagoville.[62] Then, for the second consecutive year, TBM returned to Seagoville to cook and serve a Christmas meal of roasted turkey and all the trimmings for 245 soldiers with the 341st Multifunctional Medical Battalion and their family members.[63]

Restorative Justice Ministry

As TBM became increasingly open to joining God where he seemed to be at work, the criminal justice system emerged as a major mission field. In summer 1999, two months after he joined the TBM staff to work in prison ministry, Gene Grounds was attending a conference in Austin when he heard a police sergeant from Lockhart ask a question that pierced his heart and changed his life: "Who will be there for the victim when the police leave?" Haunted by the question, Grounds began to pray for an answer, and he found it in Jesus' parable of the Good Samaritan. "The Good Samaritan showed compassion by responding to the victim's need," Grounds said. "He provided

61. Ken Camp, "TBM volunteers avert disaster by feeding military," Jan. 7, 2014, https://www.baptiststandard.com/news/texas/15967-tbm-volunteers-avert-disaster-for-event-honoring-military-personnel.

62. "Around the State: TBM feeds troops in Seagoville," Sept. 22, 2014, https://www.baptiststandard.com/news/around-the-state/16974-around-the-state-tbm-feeds-troops-in-seagoville.

63. Grace Gaddy, "TBM Military Fellowship serves Christmas dinner to soldiers and families," Dec. 11, 2014, https://www.baptiststandard.com/news/texas/17269-tbm-military-fellowship-serves-christmas-dinner-to-soldiers-and-families.

for his immediate physical needs, offered transportation and shelter, cared for the victim, spent time with him and promised to return." That parable became the model for Victim Relief Ministries, which grew out of TBM but developed into a self-sustaining interdenominational program. [64]

R.L. Barnard (right) from First Baptist Church in Duncanville and other TBM volunteers serve meals to correctional officers at the Ellis Unit.

TBM helped Victim Relief Ministries in its earliest days pilot a program in southwest Dallas involving SAVE—Serving and Assisting in Victim Emergencies—teams. Volunteers repaired broken locks and windows after burglaries, provided emergency transportation and childcare, and offered companionship to crime victims in hospitals, courtrooms and service agencies.[65] Victim Relief Ministries served about 500 crime victims during the two-year pilot program, and its Victim Chaplains Corps within the Dallas Police Department expanded citywide in 2003.[66] Victim Relief Ministries chaplains worked in New York City after the Sept. 11, 2001, terrorist attacks on the World Trade Center, ministering to rescue and recovery personnel at Ground Zero and offering critical-incident grief training for ministers in a half-dozen New York and New Jersey boroughs. In its first 10 years, Victim Relief Ministries trained more than 1,600 volunteers as victim chaplains or victim crisis responders.[67]

While Victim Relief Ministries focused on crime victims, TBM also worked to break the cycle of crime by seeking to change the lives of incarcerated individuals and their families. Every year more than 70,000 people enter the correctional system in Texas, and an equal number are released. Counting

64. Ken Camp, "Good Samaritan parable provides model for Victim Relief Ministries," Aug. 25, 2009, https://www.baptiststandard.com/news/texas/10005-good-samaritan-parable-provides-the-model-for-victim-relief-ministries.

65. Ken Camp, "Texas Baptist Men pilot project delivers aid to crime victims," Oct. 9, 2000, *Baptist Standard*, p. 2.

66. Camp, "Good Samaritan parable provides the model for Victim Relief Ministries."

67. *Ibid.*

the family members of those individuals, hundreds of thousands of people are affected. David Valentine, pastor of Covenant Fellowship in Huntsville, spoke to a TBM rally on the eve of the 2009 Baptist General Convention of Texas annual meeting, comparing the impact to a tsunami affecting 350,000 people every year. "What are you going to do about this disaster?" Valentine asked.[68]

TBM volunteers serve a meal to correctional officers inside the Wynne Unit.

At TBM's February 2012 executive board meeting and convention in Dallas, representatives from the Texas Department of Criminal Justice emphasized the difference faith-based volunteers make through discipleship programs such as Inmate Discipler Fellowship, a TBM ministry partner led by Mark Hollis. About one in four released ex-offenders in Texas return to prison within three years, but in other states of comparable size, the ratio is one out of two and sometimes two out of three, the officials said. "The difference is God," Marvin Dunbar, manager of services with the TDCJ rehabilitation programs division, told the TBM assembly, as he affirmed the role of faith-based programs and volunteers.[69] Oliver Bell, chairman of the Texas Board of Criminal Justice, noted 20,000 volunteers serve in the prison system alongside 40,000 employees—and a significant number of those volunteers serve out of a Christian commitment.

TBM Executive Director Don Gibson challenged men to join in an Experiencing God Weekend in nine Huntsville-area prisons April 27-28, 2012, and more than 100 volunteers responded to the invitation. Claude

68. John Hall, "How will Texas Baptists respond to 'tsunami' of prisoners' families?" Nov. 15, 2009, https://www.baptiststandard.com/news/texas/10380-how-will-texas-baptists-respond-to-tsunami-of-prisoners-families.

69. Ken Camp, "TBM urged to meet earth-shaking needs in criminal justice system," Feb. 23, 2012, https://www.baptiststandard.com/news/texas/13533-tbm-urged-to-meet-earth-shaking-needs-in-criminal-justice-system.

King, who wrote the *Experiencing God* curriculum with Henry Blackaby, joined that effort, meeting with inmates in the chapel of the maximum security Wynne Unit. People make bad choices, but God never fails, King told the inmates. "God is love, and God's will is the best thing for you," he said. "We can trust God's direction always to be right. It's not trial and error with God."[70] During the weekend, Valentine presented the gospel to prisoners in the Wynne Unit's administrative segregation area, where violent inmates who demonstrate they are disciplinary problems or escape risks are in solitary lock-down 23 hours a day. A pair of inmates who had moved from administrative segregation to the general prison population affirmed the impact of Valentine's ongoing ministry at the unit. Cedric, a former gang leader, accepted Christ as Lord and Savior as a result of Valentine's ministry. Cedric, in turn, led Aketa to faith in Christ, and Aketa became the first person in the state to be baptized in administrative segregation.[71]

During the weekend, Valentine introduced volunteers to an often-forgotten mission field—correctional officers. During the event, he distributed candy and water bottles to the staff. Too often, he said, the officers see faith-based volunteers walk past them without acknowledging their presence as they make their way into prisons to minister among the inmates. Correctional officers live in an "us-and them" color-coded world of uniforms, where they wear gray and inmates wear white. "The unchurched staff, in particular, see everything as gray and white. It blows their minds when they see us doing both offender ministry and officer ministry," he said.[72]

Correctional officers work in "one of the darkest places in Texas," Hollis added. It's a high-pressure environment where experience teaches officers to question motives and look at "jailhouse religion" with suspicion. "When they see the church only ministering to men in white and not the ones in gray, the officers call us 'hug-a-thugs,'" Hollis said.[73]

So, TBM responded by sponsoring a "thank you" event at the Wynne Unit during National Correctional Officers/Employees Appreciation Week in 2012. TBM volunteers cooked and served more than 600 fajita dinners for officers and their families, and they cooked an additional 150 meals they

---

70. Ken Camp, "Volunteers, inmates experience God behind prison walls," May 6, 2012, https://www.baptiststandard.com/news/texas/13766-volunteers-inmates-experience-god-behind-prison-walls.

71. *Ibid.*

72. Ken Camp, "Texas Baptists seek to minister in a world of gray and white," June 7, 2012, https://www.baptiststandard.com/news/faith-culture/13876-texas-baptists-seek-to-minister-in-a-world-of-gray-and-white.

73. *Ibid.*

left for the unit's night crew. Members of Covenant Fellowship joined in the event, distributing candy for the officers to take home to their children—a rare treat for the families on limited incomes. On the Sunday after the appreciation event, a half-dozen officers and their families attended Covenant Fellowship.

In 2015, TBM expanded its involvement in officer appreciation. Two-dozen TBM disaster relief volunteers set up a mobile kitchen outside First Baptist Church in Huntsville to cook chicken fajitas, and about 80 volunteers delivered the meals to personnel at 11 TDCJ prisons, as well as a training academy for correctional officers and a local hospital. In all, TBM fed more than 5,000—not with the biblical five loaves and two fishes, but with about 1,500 pounds of chicken and 10,000 tortillas. They also gave away about 10,000 pieces of candy and distributed more than 2,700 Bibles. In fact, requests for Bibles exceeded the number available. "To me, that represents spiritual hunger," Gibson said. "Some of the officers wanted Bibles to take home to their children or to a husband or wife."[74]

Ministry to Kurds

Another vivid example of TBM joining in God's activity—and one act of obedience leading to another—is seen in ministry to and among the Kurdish people. In the aftermath of the Gulf War in 1990-91, TBM responded to an invitation from the Office of Humanitarian Assistance in the U.S. Department of Defense, asking if the organization could provide blankets for Kurdish refugees in the mountains of western Turkey and eastern Iraq. When TBM met that need and the Dallas news media reported the story, members of the Kurdish community in Dallas visited the TBM offices to offer their thanks. The spokesmen for the Dallas Kurds—Mafa Barzani and Hashim Sushi, both Muslims—pledged their support for any future TBM ministries to the Kurds. So, when TBM subsequently sent portable field kitchens to Iran to prepare meals for Kurdish refugees, Barzani offered to accompany the team as a linguistic and cultural interpreter.

Team leader John LaNoue had his doubts. "In my experience, being short-handed on personnel and resources is not nearly as detrimental as having a team member who is not spiritually, attitudinally and morally up to the challenge," he wrote later.[75] LaNoue explained to Barzani and the other Dallas Kurds who met with TBM leaders at the Baptist Building why his

---

74. Ken Camp, "Modern feeding of the 5,000 by TBM benefits correctional officers," May 8, 2015, https://www.baptiststandard.com/news/texas/17769-modern-feeding-of-the-5-000-by-tbm-benefits-correctional-officers.

75. John LaNoue and Kaywin LaNoue, *Walking with God in Broken Places and Lessons I Learned Along the Way*, (Xulon Press: LaVerne, Tenn., 2010), p. 273.

participation in the mission was problematic. He told Barzani the team members represented Jesus Christ, and they would have to turn the other cheek if insulted. He also told Barzani the team members would gather regularly to pray, and he would be expected to join them in the prayer meetings. "I will do anything to help my people," Barzani told him.[76]

Later, an employee at the Baptist Building asked TBM Executive Director Bob Dixon if it was wise for Barzani to participate as a team member, asking, "Isn't he a Muslim?"

"Actually, he's a pre-Christian," Dixon responded.[77]

Indeed, both Barzani and Sushi became Christians. Barzani was baptized as a follower of Christ at Midway Road Baptist Church in Dallas not long after he returned from the TBM mission to Iran. Twenty years after Desert Storm, Dixon reported Barzani and Sushi continued to be involved in sharing their Christian faith with others. In fact, TBM presented its Paraboni Award, named after a first-century brotherhood of Christians who risked their lives for their faith, to the two men. "Hashim has built a swimming pool in his back yard to baptize new believers," Dixon said.[78]

TBM involvement with the Kurds continued and grew. After volunteers served at the University of Dohuk in Iraqi Kurdistan, teaching English, computers and religion, more than 60 students professed faith in Christ and were baptized—one of whom grew up to become the mayor of one of Dohuk's suburbs. In 2011, a team led by TBM volunteer Gary Smith conducted Vacation Bible Schools in churches in Kurdistan. Evangelical Christian churches exist in Dohuk, Zakho, Erbil and Sulaymaniyah, thanks in large part to TBM's ministry. "Twenty years after Desert Storm, desert showers continue," Dixon said.[79]

TBM has maintained an ongoing presence in Kurdistan for several years through Debbie Rouse, a member of Midway Road Baptist Church in Dallas, which later became Brookhaven Church in McKinney. For Rouse, answering God's call to care for widows and orphans first took her from Albania, where she worked as a TBM volunteer, to Kosovo, and eventually to Kurdistan.[80] In August 2014, the self-identified Islamic State—also known as ISIS—attacked the Yazidis and seized control of Iraq's Sinjar province.

---

76. *Ibid.*, p. 274.

77. Camp and Scott, *Anyway, Anytime, Anywhere,* pp. 174-178.

78. Undated typed note from Dixon to the author on TBM Forever Foundation letterhead, titled "20 years after Desert Storm."

79. *Ibid.*

80. Ken Camp, "Texas woman offers listening ear to grieving Kosovar," *Baptist Standard,* Sept. 22, 2000, p. 6.

Many fled, seeking refuge on Mount Sinjar. Eight months later, TBM teamed up with Brookhaven Church to collect money and essential supplies for the Yazidi refugees in Kurdistan. Once the church completed its collection, TBM volunteers loaded the supplies on pallets and filled a 40-foot shipping container.[81] The supplies included diapers, medical equipment, clothing and more than 6,700 pairs of shoes provided by Buckner International's Shoes for Orphan Souls ministry. "Our original request was for diapers and childcare items, but it just took off. God saw something bigger than we ever imagined," said Gary Smith, a member of Brookhaven Church.[82] In fact, after TBM filled the initial container, additional donations of blankets, coats, winter boots and medical supplies continued to pour in—enough to fill a second shipping container. Rouse—working with a nongovernmental organization in northern Iraq—ensured the delivery of the first container to refugees on Mount Sinjar. She distributed the supplies in three locations where she had established relationships, making certain the donated items reached the people who needed them most. The delivery took place so close to the border, she recalled, at one point her cell phone sent her a message, "Welcome to Syria." While the team visited one site, planes flew overhead, striking a nearby city four times. "I give our heavenly Father all the glory for his provisions and for safety—how he goes before me and sustains me," Rouse said. "He said he would never leave me nor forsake me, and he proves it all the time. ... Without my prayer support back home, I would not have endured it so well. I had such peace, even during the airstrikes. That peace comes only from God. I am so grateful to all who participated with me. Even though they were not physically there, I knew they were lifting me up in prayer."[83]

Ministry in Cuba

If God's invitation to ministry among the Kurds came by way of a call from the Pentagon, his invitation to minister in Cuba originated with a call from that communist government's top officials. In June 2012, an eight-member Texas Baptist Men team journeyed to Cuba at the invitation of the communist government to train Cubans in disaster relief techniques and deliver water purification equipment. The TBM volunteers not only participated in a disaster relief roundtable with government officials, but also

---

81. Grace Gaddy, "TBM to ship items for refugees in Iraq," April 9, 2015, https://www.baptiststandard.com/news/texas/17666-tbm-to-ship-items-for-refugees-in-iraq.

82. "Buckner and TBM provide hope to Yazidis in Kurdistan," Oct. 22, 2015, https://www.baptiststandard.com/news/texas/18417-buckner-and-tbm-provide-hope-to-yazidis-in-kurdistan.

83. Ken Camp, "Beautiful feet," *CommonCall*, December 2015, pp. 6-8.

made a lasting connection with leaders of the Western Baptist Convention of Cuba. In addition to providing 250 filters with 400 plastic buckets for water purification systems, the TBM team also delivered more than two dozen pairs of shoes for orphaned children on behalf of Buckner International, brought 28 duffels filled with supplies for Vacation Bible School and other children's ministries in Cuban Baptist churches, and presented 60 scholarships to students at Havana Baptist Seminary—all growing out of relationships established by L.M. Dyson, a layman at Waco's First Baptist Church of Woodway.

David Barrett from Park Cities Baptist Church works on a building project at Iglesia Bautista El Calvario in Havana.

At that point, Dyson, who served 35 years on the faculty of the Hankamer School of Business at Baylor University, had made about 30 trips to Cuba since 1999—and those trips increased in frequency after he retired. Through Dyson's contacts, TBM was invited to lead an Experiencing God Weekend at Iglesia Bautista El Calvario in downtown Havana, and he introduced TBM Executive Director Mickey Lenamon to the needs of students at Havana Baptist Seminary. Lenamon learned $200 could provide one student's room and board, tuition and books for a year, along with a travel stipend. So, TBM subsequently established the Manuel Galindo Scholarship Fund, named in honor—and in spite of the objections—of the pastor of Olmito Baptist Church in the Rio Grande Valley. Galindo is Dyson's lifelong friend, traveling companion and interpreter for nearly all his trips to Cuba. TBM raised the necessary $12,000 to provide scholarships for all the seminary's full-time resident students.[84] Four months after the trip to Cuba, TBM agreed to enter a two-year ministry partnership with the

84. Ken Camp, "Disaster relief open doors for TBM ministry in Cuba," June 26, 2012, https://www.baptiststandard.com/news/texas/13977-disaster-relief-opens-doors-for-tbm-ministry-in-cuba.

Western Baptist Convention of Cuba. The partnership was to include disaster relief training, water purification, building and remodeling projects, Royal Ambassadors leadership training, church renewal and Experiencing God weekends.[85]

Ron Wingard from Mimosa Lane Baptist Church in Mesquite uses a saw to remove a rotted area from the floor of the multi-purpose gymnasium at Iglesia Bautista El Calvario in Havana.

In 2014, TBM volunteers filled a 50-foot shipping container with supplies for Cuba. Dyson handled all the logistics of shipping and delivery, shepherding the supplies through customs, and he worked with multiple ministry partners to fill the container—one of at least two-dozen he had sent to Cuba in 15 years. "It takes so many people touching one container to get it to the right place," he said.[86] Contents included durable medical equipment collected by Woman's Missionary Union of Texas, assorted other medical supplies, disaster relief equipment for Cuban Baptists, and a washer and dryer donated by senior adults at First Baptist Church of Woodway for an elder care facility operated by the Western Baptist Convention of Cuba. The container also included three rolls of artificial turf from Baylor University, provided to the Havana Industriales baseball team for their practice facility. The Baylor baseball team developed a relationship with the professional team in Cuba during a sports evangelism trip, and at least five Industriales team members professed faith in Christ and joined Iglesia Bautista El Calvario in Havana. The shipping container also included building supplies and equipment for a remodeling job at Iglesia Bautista el Calvario in Havana. Park Cities Baptist Church in Dallas worked through the Texas Baptist Missions Foundation to provide funds to ship the container.

---

85. Ken Camp, "TBM plans partnership with Baptist in Cuba," Oct. 25, 2012, https://www.baptiststandard.com/news/texas/14421-tbm-plans-partnership-with-baptists-in-cuba.

86. Ken Camp, "Dysons deliver," *CommonCall*, March 2015, pp. 11-12.

In January 2015, a TBM missions team traveled to Cuba to unload that container and work on a construction project at Iglesia Bautista el Calvario. The TBM volunteers unloaded most of the container at the Cuban Baptist elder care home on the outskirts of Havana that received the donated

wheelchairs, walkers, crutches and other durable medical equipment. Dyson and several team members also delivered ministry supplies to a Baptist seminary in Santa Clara, a pastor in Vueltas who works with indigenous missionaries who serve about 100 sites in Central Cuba, and a pastor near Santa Clara who lives and works with his family on a demonstration farm launched through the efforts of First Baptist Church of Woodway.

Volunteers from Calvario unloaded the lumber and construction supplies at their church facility. The 113-year-old church attracts about 1,200 worshippers for services at the downtown

Mike Tello from First Baptist Church in Weslaco uses a wood chisel to remove damaged flooring from gymnasium at Iglesia Bautista El Calvario in Havana.

building, a few blocks from the nation's capitol. Typically, the church reaches an equal or greater number each week through its 114 house churches and missions. The TBM team spent several days repairing and resurfacing the floor of the gymnasium at Calvario. The church uses the gym not only for sports outreach and evangelism, but also for youth Bible study classes and various weekday ministries. Many of the same students who gather for Bible study in the gym on Sunday morning serve in the community each Sunday afternoon, feeding and bathing infirm senior adults at a state-run facility for the indigent elderly. "We have learned an important lesson from Texas Baptist Men," Pastor Juan Carlos Rojas said. "We want to demonstrate the love of God through more than words."[87]

87. Ken Camp, "In the heart of Havana, with a heart for Havana," *CommonCall*, March 2015, pp. 6-8.

One TBM volunteer, Ron Wingard from Mimosa Lane Baptist Church in Mesquite, delivered two duffels filled with children's shoes provided by Buckner International. He presented one shoe-filled bag to the administrator of the benevolence programs and women's ministries at Calvario. She told

him how much she appreciated the gift and how much good it would accomplish. Calvario's benevolence ministry not only meets needs in the congregation and in the immediate community, but also ministers throughout western Cuba. When he

Tony Garcia from First Baptist Church in Bay City works on the floor of the multi-purpose gymnasium at Iglesia Bautista El Calvario in Havana.

learned more about the scope of the ministry and depth of the need, Wingard told the administrator he had another bag of shoes available. He had planned to deliver it to the Baptist seminary in Havana, but he offered it to her, instead. "Oh, no," she said. "Take them to the seminary. Share them with them. There are so many pastors' children who don't have shoes. They have needs, too." [88]

Ministry to immigrant children

Sometimes, walking through doors God opens to meet the needs of hurting people can lead to ministry in politically sensitive and controversial places. Beginning in spring 2014, a surge of unattended minors from Central America streamed across the border into the United States without proper documentation. The Department of Homeland Security declared a level-four alert, which authorizes officials to call for resources from other agencies. The Federal Emergency Management Agency initially contacted Texas Baptist Men to request assistance in dealing with the humanitarian crisis. An unprecedented influx of unaccompanied children and teenagers—primarily

88. *Ibid.*

from El Salvador, Guatemala and Honduras—overwhelmed the ability of U.S. authorities to deal with the situation. The officials asked TBM to help provide temporary emergency childcare, showers, laundry and other services for the minors who were detained temporarily in Brownsville. "We believe this is God's invitation to us," TBM Executive Director Don Gibson reported to a meeting of the Baptist General Convention of Texas Executive Board.[89]

TBM set up a childcare unit in Brownsville, along with mobile shower and laundry units, from Second Baptist Church in LaGrange, Austin Baptist Association and Northeast Texas Disaster Response in Scroggins. Volunteers faced intensive ministry with large numbers of children for short periods of time. Regulations specified unaccompanied minors who enter the United States without documentation from countries other than Mexico had to be transferred within 72 hours to the Office of Refugee Resettlement, a division of the Department of Health and Human Services. When TBM arrived, about 400 children a day were moving through the Fort Brown Station in Brownsville before being transferred to an HHS shelter set up at Lackland Air Force Base in San Antonio. By May 28, the number spiked to 600. TBM wrapped up its large-scale mission at Fort Brown in about two weeks, washing more than 1,200 loads of laundry and making available about 1,800 showers, at which point government contractors assumed the responsibility.[90] However, TBM continued to make available laundry units as churches along the Rio Grande continued ministry throughout the summer.

Leticia Rodriguez worked as a volunteer with TBM in Brownsville, and she wrote a first-person reflection on the experience. "It broke our hearts to see their faces—small children, some scared, many not really understanding why they were here, looking totally lost and hopeless," she wrote. "Surely this could not be happening. Surely these children—and some mothers with their young ones—didn't travel thousands of miles alone, unprotected and hungry—some barefooted, some as young as 3 years old. Surely they did not leave behind loved ones but also unbearable poverty-stricken communities and rampant crime all around them. Trust me, they did. What an unbelievable and incredible situation. … Not really knowing or understanding what our mission would be upon accepting this commitment on behalf of Texas Baptist Men, God placed on our hearts to be obedient to his calling, and that we did. What an unforgettable and eye-opening experience. It's a complicated

89. Ken Camp, "TBM provides care for detained immigrant children," May 23, 2014, https://www.baptiststandard.com/news/texas/16489-tbm-provides-care-for-detained-immigrant-children.

90. Ken Camp, "TBM completes Brownsville mission to immigrant children," May 30, 2014, https://www.baptiststandard.com/news/texas/16526-tbm-volunteers-complete-brownsville-mission-to-immigrant-children.

and controversial political issue in the United States—the immigration of hundreds of children into this country. However, we did not question why they were there; we simply accepted the opportunity to tend to some of the physical and spiritual needs of these children. ... TBM representatives did their part by showing compassion, giving the children a smile and a hug, and, when the opportunity was there, to share the gospel with them. ... These little ones are wandering souls, but they are God's children."[91]

91. Leticia Rodriguez, "First Person: Little wandering souls—a desperate situation," May 23, 2014, https://www.baptiststandard.com/opinion/other/16490-first-person-little-wandering-souls-a-desperate-situation.

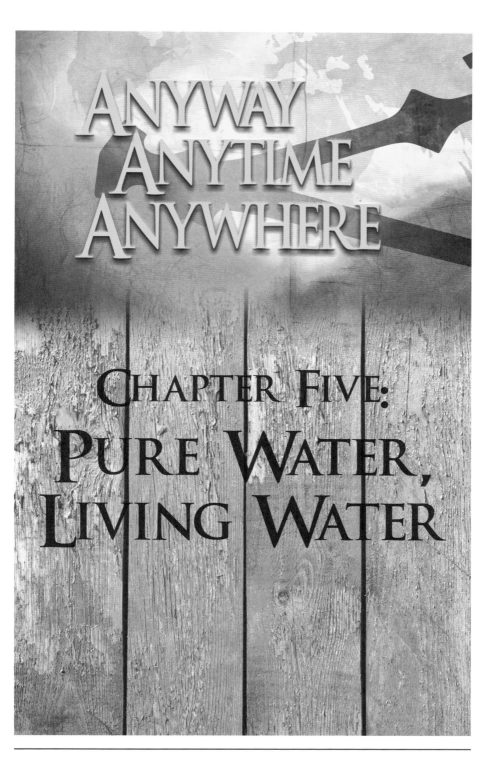

ANYWAY ANYTIME ANYWHERE

CHAPTER FIVE:
PURE WATER, LIVING WATER

CHAPTER FIVE:
PURE WATER, LIVING WATER

Texas Baptist Men volunteers long have been motivated to meet human needs out of the desire to offer "a cup of cold water" in Jesus' name. Whether providing meals, showers or laundry service to people displaced by disasters, the call to demonstrate the love of Jesus in tangible ways has driven TBM workers to the ends of the earth in service. And none of those ministries work without water.

TBM's water ministry—purifying existing water supplies, drilling wells, and teaching hygiene and sanitation—grew out of disaster relief. At least as far back as 1991, when refugees from Somalia streamed into Kenya, TBM volunteers delivered a well-drilling rig and water-purification unit to the Kenyan Baptists and taught them how to use the equipment.[92] Other disaster relief missions in the 1990s offered additional opportunities to minister through water in isolated cases. By 2000, the seeds were firmly planted for TBM's water ministry that emerged over the next decade and a half.

Mozambique and Iraq

In February and March 2000, floods caused by Cyclone Eline and a series of storms that followed forced more than 1 million people in southern Mozambique from their homes. In the process, floodwaters introduced cholera and other diseases into the water supplies. TBM representatives worked alongside volunteers from North Carolina Baptists, Oklahoma Baptists and the Baptist Union of South Africa to provide pure water for refugees in Mozambique. The team served in cooperation with the Mozambique Relief Coalition. Dick Talley, logistics coordinator for TBM, Harry Campbell from Eastside Baptist Church in Killeen and Mel Goodwin from Clarksville City Baptist Church in White Oak served on the initial team who assembled the water purification units in South Africa, after TBM discovered it would have cost more than $10,000 to ship the equipment from the United States. "I think we can build the equipment in-country," Talley said. In fact, working with an American filter company in Johannesburg, he built two units larger than any they could have transported from the United States.[93] The assembled units were then sent by helicopter to Mozambique.

---

92. Ken Camp and Orville Scott, *Anyway, Anytime, Anywhere: Thirty Years of Texas Baptist Men Ministries* (Baptist General Convention of Texas: Dallas, Texas, 1999), pp. 192-193.

93. Interview with Dick Talley in Dallas, June 12, 2015.

In Mozambique, refugees were on the move constantly from one camp to another, seeking relatives from whom they had been separated. "When they were rescued by helicopter from the rising water, they were selected on the basis of height, so children were pulled out first," Talley said. "Later, when they came back for adults, the adults may or may not have been delivered to the same camp as the children."[94]

Rex Campbell, a videographer with the BGCT communications office, and Walt Kriss, a TBM volunteer from Midway Road Baptist Church in Dallas, worked with the second team that purified water and taught local people how to operate the equipment. They operated two water purification units about 12 hours a day at a refugee camp 15 kilometers east of Chibuto, purifying at least 50,000 liters a day. They stored the purified water in two swimming pools until tanker trucks from Save the Children and Doctors Without Borders could deliver it to five refugee camps and a hospital. "The day before we left, a girl came by and told us that to her knowledge, there was not one case of cholera in any of the five camps we were serving," Kriss said.[95]

In 2003, Talley joined nine other Southern Baptist volunteers for a humanitarian mission in war-torn Iraq to install water purification units. The volunteers entered the country in a U.S. military helicopter that sustained enemy fire, and they returned to Kuwait in a C-130 cargo plane that bore the remains of four Marines killed in action. Initially, the volunteers expected to install water purification systems in remote rural villages in southern Iraq. However, when they arrived in the country, they learned the greatest need was in the hospitals of Karbala and An Najaf, south of Baghdad. "The hospitals needed safe water. Children particularly, and adults too, were getting sick from parasites that the chlorine in the water wouldn't kill," Talley said.[96]

The Baptist volunteers testified later that God provided for them each step of the way, even before they arrived in Iraq. While the crew was still in Kuwait assembling the supplies they needed, they realized they lacked granulated charcoal filters. However, Talley remembered a lesson he learned from the Mozambique mission. "Any country with a brewery, distillery or cannery had what we needed," he said.[97] Volunteers started keeping their eyes open for delivery trucks, and when they spotted a soft-drink truck, they followed it. At

---

94. "Mozambique team back; second there," *Baptist Standard*, March 22, 2000, p. 2.

95. Ken Camp, "Texas water project shows reflection of God's love," *Baptist Standard,* April 3, 2000, p. 12.

96. Ken Camp, "Texan recounts journey to provide water for Iraq," *Baptist Standard*, June 23, 2003, p. 22.

97. Interview with Talley.

the bottling plant, they talked to a supervisor, who provided all the charcoal filters they needed at no cost. Also while they were in Kuwait, they ate hamburgers at a fast-food restaurant that offered soft-sided thermal bags as a promotional giveaway. Once the crew started work in the stifling heat of Iraq, those insulated bags proved invaluable. "The Lord provided them for us," Talley said. "He knew even before we did what we needed."[98]

In Iraq, the Baptist volunteers assembled and installed five water purification units at hospitals, including two rooftop units. Before they were able to install the units, they had to remove old water tanks filled with sediment. In addition to dealing with triple-digit temperatures, the crews also discovered another challenge. The fine sand in Iraq clogged the filters. So, after they purified about 450 gallons of water, they had to flush the filters to remove the sand. Volunteers bunked alongside military personnel and shared meals-ready-to-eat with them. When they left, the Baptist crew was convinced they had opened doors for future ministry. "The hospital administrators, the mayors of the cities and everyone we worked with appreciated the fact that we didn't come in with any agendas," Talley said. "We didn't try to push anything on them. Our hearts' desire was strictly to help them, and they appreciated it."[99]

God brings key people into the ministry

The TBM water ministry reached a turning point when the organization entered into a partnership with Just Water of McKinney and its founder, Ron Mathis. Based on time-tested techniques, he developed a series of affordable and versatile ceramic filters nonprofit organizations could use with bottles, buckets, bags or bladders. In 2013, Dallas-based Ceutical Labs, a Food and Drug Administration-registered laboratory, certified the filters not only protect against bacteria, but also against viruses. Although other manufacturers of water purification products claimed their creations could remove viruses, at that point, Just Water became the first emergency water system that could back up its claim with findings from an FDA-registered laboratory.[100]

That came as no surprise to TBM. By the time the laboratory issued its finding, TBM already had been using the filters successfully around the world. In 2006, TBM learned children in villages throughout much of the Mexican state of Zacatecas were drinking water containing dangerous levels

---

98. Camp, "Texan recounts journey to provide water for Iraq."

99. *Ibid.*

100. Ken Camp, "TBM water filters confirmed to remove viruses," April 1, 2013, https://www.baptiststandard.com/news/texas/14901-tbm-water-filters-confirmed-to-remove-viruses.

of arsenic. Working with missionaries and state leaders, TBM installed a large water purifier in Santa Tomas. TBM leaders encouraged state officials to share the improved water supply with surrounding hillside villages. However, the state first had to build a new road. That led to the creation of a dam and a lake, which in turn attracted industry to a region where people previously lacked employment.[101] In 2007, TBM worked with a team of Baylor University researchers to bring water filtration to a rural village in northern Mongolia. The Baylor biologists found residents had been exposed for more than a year to toxic levels of cyanide, mercury and heavy metals such as arsenic.[102] Missionary Jerry Smith later told TBM about the impression the ministry made in the region, as expressed in the directions people gave to the clean water source: "Follow the Jesus road to where the Jesus people are working, and they will give you Jesus water."[103]

In 2009, Mathis and Talley spent two weeks in Zimbabwe, distributing 1,000 water filters, working at the request of the South African Baptist Union. Due to faulty infrastructure and a failing economy, the relentless rains that hit the capital city of Harare spread throughout the country. "The city's whole sewer system was overburdened until the point that it broke, so you can see open sewer systems flowing into gardens and trash that is not being picked up," Talley said. "The people started getting sick because they were exposed to human waste. Because Harare is the central hub of Zimbabwe, people would come into contact with cholera and take the disease back to their village."[104] While the team was in Zimbabwe, they discovered water purifiers Talley had built for Mozambique in 2000 and left in the care of the South African Baptist Union—still in use. "When you invest in water purification, it's not a one-time gift. It keeps giving year after year," Talley said. "We didn't just give them clean water to drink. We taught them how to make clean water for themselves. And that was more beneficial."[105]

In addition to Mathis, God brought along another key figure in the development of TBM's water ministry. Bob Young from The Heights Baptist

101. Barbara Bedrick, "Texas Baptist Men seek to provide pure Water of Life," Dec. 29, 2006, https://www.baptiststandard.com/resources/archives/46-2006-archives/5978-texas-baptist-men-seek-to-provide-pure-water-of-life.

102. Matt Pene, "Baylor and Texas Baptist Men bring clean water to Mongolian town," Nov. 30, 2007, https://www.baptiststandard.com/resources/archives/47-2007-archives/7276-baylor-and-texas-baptist-men-bring-clean-water-to-mongolian-town.

103. "TBM volunteers recount 'activity of God,'" March 5, 2009, https://www.baptiststandard.com/news/texas/9255-tbm-volunteers-recount-activity-of-god.

104. Crystal Donahue, "TBM provides pure water, living water in Zimbabwe," June 11, 2009, https://www.baptiststandard.com/news/texas/9657-tbm-provides-pure-water-living-water-in-zimbabwe.

105. *Ibid.*

Church in Richardson initially became involved with TBM through disaster relief, hoping to ease into the ministry gradually. "I wanted a nice little entry-level disaster," he said. Instead, he served in the days immediately after Hurricane Katrina and Hurricane Rita. The twin hurricanes that hit in August and September 2005 were the costliest disaster—and one of the most widespread and deadly—in U.S. history. "That was my first rodeo,"[106] he said. Before long, he became involved with the water ministry, and TBM leaders asked him to lead the effort "on a trial basis."

Bob Young from The Heights Baptist Church in Richardson uses simple manual tools to drill a well.

In the years that followed, Young traveled to some of the poorest favelas in Brazil, the most primitive villages along the Amazon and the most crowded tent cities in China. In 2012, Sandy Wisdom-Martin, executive director-treasurer of Woman's Missionary Union of Texas, contacted Young to ask about drilling water wells in Ghana. Young told her TBM focused on water purification. By this time, TBM had expanded the ministry to more than 70 countries, and an estimated 90 million gallons of water a year was being purified through the water filters TBM distributed to people in need. TBM lacked the expertise and equipment to drill wells, he explained. However, Wisdom-Martin learned about Water for All International, a ministry led by Terry Waller from Southland Baptist Church in San Angelo. The ministry used simple tools available in nearly any country and low-cost methods to equip poor families to drill their own wells. So, Texas WMU used funds from the Mary Hill Davis Offering for Texas Missions to send

---

106. Ken Camp, "Together in Missions," *CommonCall,* July 2013, pp. 16-17.

TBM representatives to San Angelo to learn the well-drilling technique and subsidized half the cost of sending a TBM team to Ghana to do the work. Young journeyed to Ghana with two other TBM volunteers—Roy Heflin from Cowboy Church of Ellis County and Dale Moore from Mayfield Road

Baptist Church in Arlington. The trio drilled about 47 feet deep in nine days at the site of a seminary that was under construction in Tamale. The drilling rig consisted of a 12- to 14-foot tripod, a 50-foot rope draped over a large pulley and a spring-steel bit on a 5-foot pipe. [107]

In 2013, Harold Patterson from Scroggins participated in a TBM water ministry mission well-drilling trip to Kenya. The volunteers wanted to use appropriate technology the local residents could replicate and maintain. However, the hand-operated auger they tried to use hit hard shale

Harold Patterson from Scroggins built a small-scale water well-drilling rig using a simple two-person posthole digger and a six-horsepower engine. (Photo / David Clanton)

and could not penetrate it. The team had to complete the well with picks and shovels. Patterson had more than three and half decades experience as an auto mechanic, and he also had worked on an oil well-drilling rig many years earlier. Drawing on that base of knowledge, he built a small-scale water well-

107. Ken Camp, "TBM, WMU partnership empowers poor in Ghana to drill water wells," July 25, 2012, https://www.baptiststandard.com/news/texas/14088-tbm-wmu-partnership-empowers-poor-in-ghana-to-drill-water-wells.

drilling rig using a simple two-person posthole digger and a six-horsepower engine. He built the first rig for less than $2,000. Don Gibson asked him about building five rigs if God provided $10,000. Within a few weeks, before the need was widely publicized, he already had received $8,000.[108] Working with Phil Davenport from First Baptist Church in Garland, Patterson and his wife, Kathy, drilled wells at a seminary and church in Nigeria at the request of Mary Kay and Fred Posey, leaders of Walking in Love Ministries. "We left the well-drilling rig there and trained a team of Nigerians how to use and maintain it," Patterson said. "Before we left, two chiefs came with requests for 10 more locations for the team to start drilling." [109]

TBM volunteers subsequently drilled a water well for Leishiphung Christian Hospital in the Himalayas of Manipur, India. After five failed attempts, the rig—previously believed to have a maximum drilling depth of 100 feet— drilled through 70 feet of hard shale before reaching water at 120 feet. [110] During summer 2015, Patterson and other TBM water ministry volunteers taught 11 indigenous missionaries from Venzuela how to drill water wells and maintain a drilling rig. The Venezuelans—enlisted by Paul Lozuk, who grew up as a missionary kid in Venezuela and returned there several years ago—successfully drilled a 45-foot water well and poured a concrete pad around the casing at the Everything Jesus Ranch near Seguin, where they trained.[111]

God brought another key individual into the water ministry when Dee Dee Wint from The Village Church in Flower Mound joined the team. In November 2015, she traveled to Nigeria with the Poseys to teach lifesaving sanitation and hygiene lessons. At the February 2016 TBM board meeting, she reported in Africa, 2,000 children a day die from dehydration due to water-related diseases, and 90 percent of those deaths are preventable. She described the oral rehydration therapy method TBM had started teaching in developing nations. Using a small plastic spoon with a scoop at each end, volunteers teach families how to measure precise amounts of sugar and salt, and then add them to purified water they drink to replace bodily fluids lost due to diarrhea. "It gives people a way they can take control of their own

---

108. Ken Camp, "Equipped to help," *Common Call*, August 2014, pp. 6-10.

109. Ken Camp, "TBM volunteers drill wells in Nigeria," Nov. 5, 2014, https://www. baptiststandard.com/news/texas/17134-tbm-volunteers-drill-wells-in-nigeria.

110. Ken Camp, "Water ministry provides showers of blessings globally, TBM board learns," Feb. 27, 2015, https://www.baptiststandard.com/news/texas/17517-water- ministry-provides-showers-of-blessings-globally-tbm-board-learns.

111. Ken Camp, "TBM volunteers train indigenous missionaries from Venezuela," July 30, 2015, https://www.baptiststandard.com/news/texas/18110-tbm-volunteers-train- indigenous-missionaries-from-venezuela.

health," Wint explained. "And all the time we are teaching them about it, we are also teaching them the love of Jesus Christ."[112]

In November 2016, Wint and her husband, Tim, and Billy Joe Wall, pastor of Avenue Baptist Church in Hereford, spent two weeks in Sierra Leone. The TBM team drilled and installed wells and taught health and hygiene classes, working in cooperation with the Konoyima Educational Fund. They served in the Kono District, an area where 70 percent of the people live below the poverty line. About half the men and three-fourths of the women are illiterate. The Konoyima Educational Fund started Christian schools and churches throughout the region, but many were in an area lacking access to clean water, and the district was experiencing an 80 percent infant mortality rate due to water-borne diseases. In two villages, the TBM team drilled two wells at least 40 feet deep, tapping into an aquifer far below polluted groundwater seepage. Wall worked more than three decades in the well-drilling business before he became a Baptist camp manager and finally accepted his first pastorate at age 63. In addition to applying his well-drilling expertise, Wall also preached at two Sunday worship services at churches in Sierra Leone. Wint trained 27 church leaders, who in turn led classes in two villages. At one of the health and hygiene classes led in a community center by church leaders, 209 people attended. Seventy-five made professions of faith in Christ, including seven women from Muslim homes.[113]

---

112. Ken Camp, "TBM board hears reports on far-flung ministries," Feb. 24, 2016, https://www.baptiststandard.com/news/texas/18829-tbm-board-hears-reports-on-far-flung-ministries.

113. Ken Camp, "TBM offers pure water and Living Water to Sierra Leone," Nov. 30, 2016, https://www.baptiststandard.com/news/texas/19768-tbm-offers-pure-water-and-living-water-to-sierra-leone.

ANYWAY ANYTIME ANYWHERE

CHAPTER SIX:
NATURAL TRAGEDIES AND MANMADE TERROR

CHAPTER SIX:
NATURAL TRAGEDIES AND
MANMADE TERROR

A year and a half after he retired from his TBM staff position—and after months involving surgery for cancer, radiation treatments and chemo-hormone injections—John LaNoue journeyed to New York in the aftermath of the 9/11 terrorist attacks. He served as the manager of the Southern Baptist disaster relief base. Southern Baptist volunteers focused on providing meals for workers, assisting the Salvation Army with staff for a kitchen at Ground Zero, and caring for the 150 Baptist volunteers a week who arrived to help with clean-up. (Photo / David Clanton)

Texas Baptist Men disaster relief volunteers began the new century and the new millennium by building on a solid foundation. TBM had blazed the trail among Southern Baptists in disaster relief ministry. The ministry grew from humble beginnings— Bob Dixon cooking meals for victims of Hurricane Beulah over a couple of homemade "buddy burners" in 1967. It gained momentum after John LaNoue built the first disaster relief mobile unit with its self-contained field kitchen in his home driveway. Other Baptist state conventions modeled disaster relief programs after what TBM created, and a nationwide network developed— first coordinated by the Southern Baptist Convention's Brotherhood Commission and later by the North American Mission Board. By the early 2000s, TBM maintained a fleet of vehicles, including specialized trailers for shower and laundry service, temporary emergency childcare, mud-out after floods and other ministries. Equally significant, TBM had trained and equipped volunteers across the state to respond in Jesus' name when disasters hit.

Earthquake in El Salvador

Late in 2000, TBM volunteers worked two weeks in Northeast Texas, where they served 51,200 meals to people who had been affected by an ice storm. Just a few weeks later, volunteers responded to the call after an earthquake rocked El Salvador. The quake on Jan. 13, 2001, its aftershocks and the resultant landslides claimed more than 900 lives, destroyed more than 100,000 homes and damaged an even greater number. A three-member TBM advance team arrived in El Salvador Jan. 20. Gary Smith of Dallas, Eddie Fonseca of Canyon Lake and Harry Campbell of Killeen went to work purchasing and assembling equipment for field kitchens. The next day, nine other TBM volunteers joined them, and they divided into two six-member crews to establish field kitchens at separate locations. Smith led a crew that established emergency food service in Lourdes, a remote mountainous area about 30 kilometers from San Salvador, where they served about 2,000 people twice daily within a few days after setting up operations. On the second day the volunteers served food, 35 people who were waiting in the serving lines made professions of faith in Christ. Jered Sellers of Plains led the second team, who set up a field kitchen near Santa Tecla, at the El Cafetalon soccer field, where displaced people lived in a tent city. The crew served about 4,000 people at each evening meal.[114]

During their time in El Salvador, the TBM volunteers noted multiple occasions when God answered prayers to meet urgent needs. When Smith initially set up the field kitchen in Lourdes, one of the first arrangements he made was to have a water line installed. However, when the crew turned on three faucets, all three were dry. Although local officials promised to remedy the situation, it appeared doubtful they would be able to take care of it in time for the first evening meal. So, the crew gathered to pray, asking God to provide. "He provided, just in the knick of time," Smith recalled. "A truck and bladder of water arrived just in time for us to get the meal ready."[115]

On another occasion, the TBM crew ran out of fruit and vegetables to serve. Again, the crew prayed. Once again, a truck arrived, driven by several Guatemalan pastors who delivered fruit and vegetables. One of the pastors told Smith the Lord had told them to come. "We had a complete sense that

114. Ken Camp, "Texas Baptist Men are cooking now in El Salvador," *Baptist Standard*, Jan. 29, 2001, p. 12.

115. Ken Camp, "Volunteers witness miraculous provision amid rubble of El Salvador earthquake," *Baptist Standard*, Feb. 12, 2001, p. 1.

the Lord was with us," Smith said. "It was so clear that he was there, and we were doing what he wanted us to do. We would pray, and the answer would always come. It was like we had a hotline." [116]

Apparently, the hotline to God did not run exclusively from Lourdes, because the crew at El Cafetalon reported similar experiences. Fonseca recalled an occasion when the volunteers felt certain God "multiplied" one pot of boiling water far beyond any reasonable limit. "One day, we were at our peak, serving 16,000 meals," he said. "We boiled 8,000 eggs, turned around and used the same water to boil 8,000 potatoes, then used that same water to cook rice. It was like the loaves and the fishes, except it was 16,000 instead of 5,000."[117]

God also provided financial resources when the crews needed them most urgently. Sellers recalled a time when his team ran out of money to buy groceries, and they asked God to supply what they needed. A man from California showed up at the TBM campsite, offering to help. Initially, Sellers eyed him with suspicion. "But I saw him wiping noses and doing things a lot of people wouldn't do," he recalled, and that convinced him the man's heart was in the right place. That opinion was solidified when the Californian learned about the crew's funding shortage and donated $4,000 over the course of three days. "God taught me a lesson about judging people," Sellers acknowledged.[118]

In less than two weeks in El Salvador, the two TBM crews prepared more than 100,000 meals. They also led an estimated 200 or more people to faith in Christ, including a captain in the Mexican army and his chief aide and a volunteer from Panama who worked alongside the Texas volunteers. "Only the Lord will know the final tally," Fonseca said.[119]

Tropical Storm Allison

In early June 2001, Tropical Storm Allison inundated Southeast Texas, claiming more than 40 lives and damaging more than 70,000 homes. The storm hit Houston particularly hard, including the city's massive Texas Medical Center district. TBM volunteers responded to the need, setting up a field kitchen in a parking lot behind the Edwin Hornberger Building at the medical center. Working in sweltering heat and humidity, TBM crews provided meals for some patients and nearly all the staff at Methodist Hospital and St. Luke's Episcopal Hospital. They also cooked meals for the

---

116. *Ibid.*
117. *Ibid.*
118. *Ibid,* p.12.
119. *Ibid.*

staff at Memorial Hermann Hospital, which had to evacuate patients and suspend operations at one point. The TBM volunteers also provided meals for security officers and administration at the Texas Medical Center and the Harris County Medical Examiner's Office. Meanwhile, other TBM crews set up food-service operations at First Baptist Church in Humble, First Baptist Church of Deer Park and other locations.[120]

In three weeks, TBM volunteers cooked more than 326,000 meals. Local volunteers—including 32 Buddhist monks, on one occasion—joined the TBM crews. Baptists who worked in the oppressive heat over boiling pots included multiple senior adults, one heart transplant recipient and a legally blind individual. "Watching these people just reminded me once again that no one has any excuse for not serving God," John LaNoue said.[121] The long, hot summer in Houston prepared TBM for a call to service in September nobody anticipated—and all involved prayed they never would experience again.

Ministry in New York after 9/11

A year and a half after he retired from his staff post at TBM—and after months involving surgery for cancer, radiation treatments and chemo-hormone injections—John LaNoue admittedly didn't rise as early each morning as he once did. So, he was still reclining in bed on Sept. 11, 2011, when he received a troubling call from his daughter, Lydia, in New Jersey. She told her father an airplane had just flown into the World Trade Center. Like many people who heard the initial report, LaNoue first assumed a small private plane had lost its bearings and hit the building. While the pair still talked on the phone, Lydia watched on television as another airliner crash into the second of the twin towers. As events continued to unfold that morning—including the airplane that struck the Pentagon and the fourth plane that crashed into a field in Pennsylvania—LaNoue called the TBM office to find out if disaster relief volunteers were being mobilized. At that point, he learned, TBM disaster relief was on alert but volunteers had not been activated, since leaders had not yet received a request from the North American Mission Board. Since LaNoue had worked directly with NAMB, he called Director Mickey Caison to say he and his wife, Kaywin, were available. "Pack your bags, and come to Atlanta. I need you both in the disaster volunteer center," Caison said.[122] The couple worked for a week in Atlanta, enlisting and organizing response teams, before Caison asked them

120. Ken Camp, "Texas Baptist Men roll into rain-soaked Houston," *Baptist Standard*, June 18, 2001, p. 8.

121. Ken Camp and Karen Simons, "Thousands of volunteers needed in Houston," *Baptist Standard*, July 9, 2001, p. 1.

122. John and Kaywin LaNoue, *Walking with God in Broken Places* (Xulon Press: LaVerne, Tenn., 2010), p. 394.

to return to Texas and pack their motor home for an extended stay in New York City.

After a long journey to New York, the LaNoues set up their motor home at the Brooklyn Naval Yards, where NAMB had established its base of disaster relief operations. The multi-state Southern Baptist response involved a mobile field kitchen, a laundry unit and a shower unit. For the most part, the Southern Baptist volunteers focused on providing meals for workers, assisting the Salvation Army with staff for a kitchen at Ground Zero, and caring for the 150 Baptist volunteers a week who arrived to help with clean-up. Caison named LaNoue manager of the Baptist disaster base and then gave him a special assignment, based on a request from Mayor Rudolph Giuliani. Baptists in Oklahoma City who had ministered in the wake of the Murrah Federal Building bombing had received a significant number of teddy bears they gave to children who were affected by the tragedy in their city. They wanted to do the same for New York. When word spread, others joined the effort, and the New York mayor's office soon had a warehouse filled with more than 40,000 teddy bears—and more arriving daily. So, Caison enlisted LaNoue to handle the proliferating teddy bear problem.

"We selected a team of six bear handlers, rented a Ryder truck and began taking teddy bears out of the warehouses in New York and New Jersey," LaNoue later recalled.[123] After bringing the stuffed bears back to the disaster relief base for sorting, they began distributing them to fire stations, police stations and the Victims Family Service Center. They also provided them to hospital pediatric wards and to EMS personnel for their ambulances to use on calls involving children. "The impact of the teddy bear ministry opened doors for witnessing, spiritual counseling and a ministry of prayer that would have been absolutely impossible otherwise," LaNoue said.[124]

In addition to the hundreds of thousands of meals TBM volunteers helped other Southern Baptist disaster relief volunteers prepare and the countless teddy bears distributed throughout New York City, Victim Relief Ministries also served in the wake of 9/11. Chaplains offered prayer and spiritual counsel to rescue and recovery personnel who worked at Ground Zero. They also provided critical-incident grief training for more than 300 ministers and others in a half-dozen boroughs.[125]

---

123. *Ibid.*, p. 398.

124. *Ibid.*, p. 402.

125. Ken Camp, "Good Samaritan parable provides the model for Victim Relief Ministries," *Baptist Standard*, Aug. 25, 2009, p. 3.

Myriad ministries on multiple fronts

While some TBM volunteers still were participating in the multi-state disaster relief effort in New York, others began a widespread response at multiple sites—in Texas, around the United States and globally—that extended for months. In mid-October, volunteers from Tarrant Baptist Association went to work in Hondo, providing up to 5,000 meals a day for residents living in the aftermath of a tornado that tore through the Hill Country community west of San Antonio. About that same time, TBM responded to a request from the Southern Baptist International Mission Board for help in Belize, where Hurricane Isis swept through the southern part of the country, leaving at least 13,000 people homeless. Missionary Ken Moore reported the hurricane destroyed two Baptist church buildings and left at least 40 member families homeless in the Bella Vista, Silver Creek and San Pedro Columbia villages. TBM made available funds to provide temporary shelters for homeless families and mobilized crews to build permanent homes and churches.[126]

A few months later, TBM chainsaw crews responded to a request for help from the Baptist Convention of New Mexico. In April, wildfires threatened the Sivells Baptist Retreat and Conference Center in the Sacramento Mountains of south Central New Mexico. The fires destroyed 12 cabins and two bathhouses, but the main buildings escaped unharmed. However, since the dense forests around the conference center burned, the erosion control the undergrowth provided was lost. That left the encampment in danger of flooding. So, in May, the TBM crews cut down charred trees to create dams and berms to hold the soil in place and channel rainwater away.[127]

A few weeks later, TBM volunteers began an extensive response to wildfires in Colorado. In mid-June, the Top O'Texas disaster relief crew served three meals a day to victims of the Iron Mountain fire in central Colorado who had to evacuate their homes. The 15-member team prepared the meals for displaced families at First Southern Baptist Church in Cañon City, southwest of Colorado Springs, and also delivered them to firefighters battling the blaze about 50 miles away. "They were able to minister to those who lost basically everything—their clothes, their house, their vehicles," said Morgan Kerr, pastor of the Cañon City church. "They were able to provide basic needs for them."[128] Several members of the same team later relocated to the Douglas

---

126. Ken Camp, "Texas Baptist Men work on three fronts," *Baptist Standard*, Oct. 22, 2001, p. 2.
127. Ken Camp, "Texas Men working from New Mexico to Gaza Strip," *Baptist Standard*, May 27, 2002, p. 12.
128. John Hall, "Texas Baptist Men offer assistance to victims of Colorado's wildfires," *Baptist Standard,* June 17, 2002, p. 2.

County Fairgrounds in Castle Rock, where the Hayman fire south of Denver forced the evacuation of 7,500 homes. "You get the opportunity to witness to people in distress," said Tim Willis of First Baptist Church in Plains. "You get to help people."[129]

As wildfires continued to plague the West, TBM responded next in Arizona, where the Rodeo-Chediski fire engulfed 409,000 acres and forced the evacuation of 30,000 people. TBM crews served about 2,000 meals a day in late June, supporting an aid camp located about 45 miles east of the fire line. "We're helping people in need. We're giving a cool glass of water in the name of Jesus," said Robert Thomas, a TBM volunteer from Main Street Baptist Church in Grand Saline. "We're feeding those who cannot feed themselves at this point."[130]

Soon, the TBM disaster relief ministry was stretched to maximum capacity when, in addition to ongoing ministry to Arizona and Colorado residents displaced by fires, volunteers also sought to minister to Texas residents affected by floods that reached from Abilene to Victoria. As floods that began in the Central Texas Hill Country started draining southeastward toward the Gulf, more rain fell, compounding the problem and covering a landmass roughly equal in size to the state of Oklahoma. For the first time since TBM established its network of regional disaster relief ministries, every disaster relief unit in the state was called into service at the same time. Nine regional units—along with the statewide mobile unit, command post and emergency child-care trailer—operated from July 12 to 18, before four units were released. TBM established emergency food service operations in San Antonio, New Braunfels, Uvalde, Abilene, Brownwood, Sattler, Kerrville, Bandera, Mathis and Victoria, preparing more than 77,000 meals. Mud-out crews provided more than 10,000 hours of labor, helping residents clean out their homes and small businesses.[131] Two units that had been serving in Arizona were called back to Texas to serve in Abilene and Brownwood. In spite of the logistical challenges created by the widespread response, volunteers maintained a positive attitude, seeing it as a unique opportunity for ministry. "There's something about a disaster situation that softens their heart," said Jered Sellers from Plains. "God breaks down the walls in their heart, and the chance to minister to them is multiplied. ... God's getting us ready for something. God's preparing us to do his work through disaster relief."[132]

129. John Hall, "Texas Baptist Men still serving on edge of Colorado wildfires," *Baptist Standard*, June 24, 2002, p. 2.

130. John Hall, "Fired up for service," *Baptist Standard*, July 1, 2002, pp. 1, 12.

131. Ken Camp, "Disaster relief work stretched thin as floodwaters spread," *Baptist Standard*, July 22, 2002, p. 1.

132. John Hall, "Out of the fire & into the flood," *Baptist Standard,* July 15, 2002, pp. 1, 7.

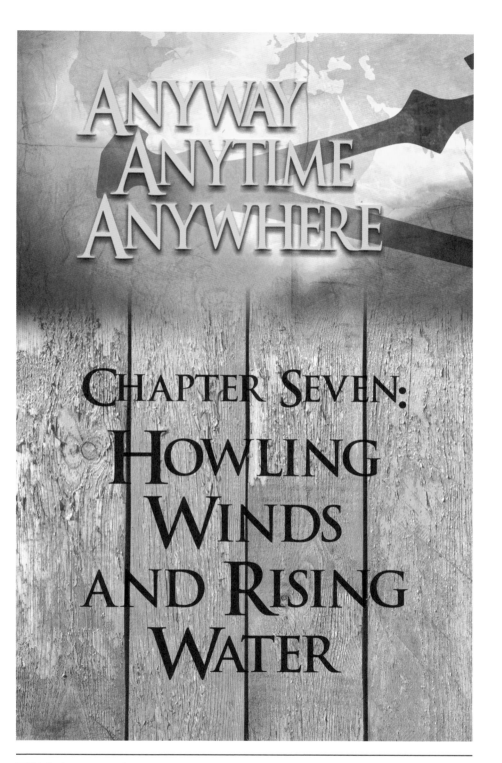

ANYWAY
ANYTIME
ANYWHERE

CHAPTER SEVEN:
HOWLING
WINDS
AND RISING
WATER

CHAPTER SEVEN:
HOWLING WINDS AND RISING WATER

Space Shuttle Columbia Recovery

As needs continued to multiply and events called TBM to an ever-widening circle of involvement, God expanded the organization's ability to respond by providing additional equipment.

Hopes and dreams fell to Earth at 8 a.m. Feb. 1, 2003. The space shuttle Columbia broke apart during re-entry on its 28th mission, killing all seven crew members. Its debris field spanned hundreds of miles of the East Texas Pineywoods, and public safety officers began the grim duty of recovery. The day after the disaster, Texas Baptist Men volunteers served 1,500 meals to law enforcement officers and other searchers who scoured the woods and pastures of Nacogdoches County, and they served an equal number the next day. A TBM crew set up a self-contained field kitchen on the grounds of the Nacogdoches County Expo Center, which served as a staging area for Highway Patrol with the Texas Department of Public Safety, Texas Rangers, sheriff's deputies and other law officers. "We made hot coffee for the DPS 24/7," TBM volunteer Gary Smith recalled years later. And as the temperature continued to drop, it became even more welcomed by the troopers. "We made the coffee in 33-gallon steam kettles," he said. Within a couple of days, TBM disaster relief volunteers from the Hill Country arrived with a shower and laundry trailer.[133]

The TBM disaster relief volunteers worked in close partnership with chaplains from Victim Relief Ministries, who sought to provide comfort and spiritual support to searchers who not only discovered metal fragments

---

133. Interview with Gary Smith, Dallas, Oct. 2, 2015.

from the shuttle, but also found scattered remains of its crew. The chaplains set up a trailer at the Expo Center to offer a "ministry of presence" for searchers. "When the Highway Patrol come to the Expo Center for their assignments or to the disaster relief unit to eat, we're there just to visit with them, talk to them and make sure they're OK," said Mike Brittain of Diana, who coordinated the team. The chaplains also organized a Sunday evening worship service in the Expo Center rodeo arena for any searchers who wanted to attend, and some officers also joined the chaplains for their morning devotionals. Other Texas Baptists joined the searchers in the field. Fred Raney, pastor of First Baptist Church in Hemphill, worked with the crews in the Angelina and Sabine national forests, near the Louisiana border. Raney, who served with the Hemphill Volunteer Fire Department, worked as a chaplain, offering spiritual counsel and prayer to searchers tasked with the grim responsibility of recovering body parts.[134]

Chaplains also quietly made their presence known at the Johnson Space Center during a Feb. 4 memorial service. A half-dozen Victim Relief Ministries chaplains attended the service, where President George W. Bush offered words of comfort to grieving family members and their friends. "You are not alone," Bush said. "In time, you will find comfort and grace to see you through. And in God's own time, we can pray that the day of your reunion will come." Other chaplains staffed a tent designated as a "prayer center" at the entrance to the facility. During the memorial service, visitors outside the gate stood in silent reverence, watching the tribute on four television monitors. "Afterward, people wanted to share their thoughts," Brittain recalled. "They wanted to reflect on the service and talk about how meaningful it was to them." One woman, who identified herself as the wife of an astronaut, hugged Brittain's neck and asked for prayer, telling him how difficult the experience was for her and her teenaged daughter. Several times, Brittain gently approached people who stood at the gate weeping. "I'd just put my arm around them, let them know they're loved and tell them, 'I'll pray for you,'" he said. "We're just trying to touch the people and let them know we are here for them."[135]

Time of expansion

As needs continued to multiply in 2003 and events called TBM to an ever-widening circle of involvement, God expanded the organization's ability to respond by providing additional equipment. The Texas Baptist Missions

---

134. Ken Camp, "After shuttle fell, Texas Baptists served up love," *Baptist Standard,* Feb. 10, 2003, p. 8.

135. Ken Camp, "Bush offers words of comfort at NASA memorial," *Baptist Standard*, Feb. 10, 2003, p. 8.

Foundation took the lead in raising $30,000 to purchase an emergency response tool trailer for TBM, which brought the total number of rolling stock to 35, including vehicles and trailers owned by churches and associations throughout Texas. The trailer provided TBM a place to store and transport tools that would allow volunteers to repair churches, encampments and other facilities damaged by disasters.[136] Within a few weeks, the fleet continued to increase in size, when Austin Baptist Association added a mobile laundry unit. Churches and individuals in the Austin area financed construction of the custom-made 16-foot tandem-axle trailer with three washing machines, three dryers, an on-board generator and a supply of propane. TBM also secured a 48-foot box trailer that was converted to a "rolling bunkhouse" that could provide on-site lodging for up to 16 volunteers during a disaster relief mission.[137]

TBM disaster relief volunteers responded to multiple incidents of flooding in 2003 and 2004. In late September, 2003, a 10-member team from Wichita-Archer-Clay Baptist Association and from East Texas journeyed to Middle River, Md., to provide emergency food service in an area that suffered from flooding and power outages after Hurricane Isabel. As part of a multi-state response, the TBM volunteers prepared about 16,000 meals in the first four days in Maryland.[138] A couple of months later, floodwaters threatened the single mothers and their children at Gracewood in Houston, a ministry of what was then known as Texas Baptist Children's Home & Family Services, now Children at Heart Ministries. "The water came up so quickly that we barely had time to react," Gracewood Executive Director Mike Hammack said. "We immediately shut off the electricity and gas and started evacuating the families." When they returned, they found devastation, but they also found help in 10 TBM disaster relief volunteers from Austin and LaGrange and about 40 from a Houston church. The volunteers removed water-damaged drywall and then pressure-washed and disinfected surfaces.[139]

The following May, some of those same volunteers from LaGrange responded to another disaster, when Robertson County received 17 inches of rain in less than nine hours. Larry Blackmon, pastor of First Baptist

136. Ken Camp, "Texas Baptist Men's disaster relief fleet expands to 35 vehicles," Sept. 19, 2003, https://www.baptiststandard.com/resources/archives/43-2003-archives/898-tbmrelief92203.

137. Ken Camp, "Texas Baptist Men respond far & wide," Oct. 3, 2003, https://www.baptiststandard.com/resources/archives/43-2003-archives/959-tbmdisasters10603.

138. *Ibid.*

139. "Houston flooding sweeps ministry's residents into sudden evacuation," Dec. 5, 2003, https://www.baptiststandard.com/resources/archives/43-2003-archives/1287-houston-flooding-sweeps-ministrys-residents-into-sudden-evacuation120803.

Church in Hearne, was among the residents affected by the flooding, which damaged about 200 homes. Later, Blackmon recalled watching furniture float in his swamped home and helping his grandchildren escape rising water by lifting them through a window to a man driving a tractor by his home. But Blackmon—and residents of 15 other homes—received help from the LaGrange mud-out team who pulled up soaked carpet, ripped up warped baseboards and removed damaged sheetrock. A TBM childcare team provided a safe environment for children as their parents worked in flood-damaged homes. Other TBM volunteers worked throughout the night at the First Baptist Church parsonage, separating and sorting drenched photographs from family albums, and helping the Blackmons reclaim sentimental treasures. Instead of preaching the following Sunday, Blackmon turned the worship service over to the TBM volunteers, allowing them to share their testimonies about how and why they became involved in the disaster relief ministry.[140]

Early in 2004, TBM also responded internationally, after a massive earthquake left three-fourths of the ancient city of Bam, Iran, in ruins. The Texas volunteers knew they were following an Alabama Baptist team, but they had no idea until they arrived how the earlier crew had paved the way for them. Since "Ala" sounded like the Iranian word for God, "ba" like "with" and "ma" like "us," the group became identified locally as "God with us." TBM team leader John LaNoue recalled the cold reception his crew received from a stern government worker when they first arrived, but the official immediately warmed to them when he learned they were related to the "Ala-ba-ma" group. The TBM team worked in a 341-tent refugee camp that housed more than 1,700 people. The disaster relief crew cooked more than 3,000 meals and 5,000 cups of hot tea each day for the camp, plus an additional 1,000 meals daily for another nearby camp. Volunteers worked 14-hour days, cooking rice, lentils and occasional helpings of lamb. Although the crew included one 36-year-old volunteer and a 41-year-old physician, the average age was 63, and the oldest volunteer was 78. LaNoue learned from an interpreter many of the people in the camp asked: "Why have these old men come to help us? We see them working when we get up in the morning and working when we go to bed at night."[141] Although the team members had to be careful not to be perceived by authorities as proselytizing, they were free to identify themselves as Christians when asked—including

---

140. John Hall, "Flood leaves pastor praising God for volunteers," https://www.baptiststandard.com/resources/archives/44-2004-archives/1944-flood-leaves-pastor-praising-god-for-volunteers53104.

141. Ken Camp, "TBM volunteers glad Alabama group paved the way in Iran relief," Jan. 27, 2004, https://www.baptiststandard.com/resources/archives/44-2004-archives/1468-tbm-volunteers-glad-alabama-group-paved-the-way-in-iran-relief12604.

by authorities who interviewed them up to three times a day, asking why they came to Iran. "My prayer for the people of Iran is that they will have the opportunity to recognize the truth, that God will bless them with the knowledge of himself, (and) that their physical needs will be met in such a way that they will come to recognize the giver of good gifts," LaNoue said later.

Summer 2004 offered additional opportunities for service to survivors of floods in North Texas. In June, TBM dispatched disaster relief crews to the area surrounding Fort Worth. Mud-out and clean-up crews worked in White Settlement, and TBM volunteers assisted Salvation Army workers in Parker County. The Tarrant Baptist Association emergency food service unit set up a field kitchen at Weatherford College and worked to support the Parker County Service Center.[142] In August, TBM mud-out crews worked in southern Dallas County. Volunteers removed furniture, helped residents pack their belongings for storage, and removed water-soaked sheetrock from flooded homes. The Dallas Baptist Association emergency food-service unit prepared about 600 meals a day for the American Red Cross to deliver to people in need. Members of First Baptist Church in Lancaster and Hampton Road Baptist Church in DeSoto worked with the food-service team, volunteers from The Oaks Baptist Church in Grand Prairie helped the mud-out crews and a youth group from Cliff Temple Baptist Church in Dallas helped residents pack and store their possessions.[143]

TBM disaster relief volunteers spent the next couple of months in Florida and Alabama in the wake of Hurricane Frances and in Grenada after Hurricane Ivan swept through the Caribbean. Multiple Texas chainsaw, clean-up, building and food-service crews joined other Southern Baptist disaster relief volunteers in the multi-state response in the Southeast. In the immediate aftermath of Hurricane Frances, six million Florida residents lost electricity, and more than 74,000 were housed in emergency shelters.[144] Teams arrived in Mobile, Ala., which served as their staging area until they received assignments elsewhere. The volunteers' ministry in Florida was interrupted when Hurricane Ivan approached, prompting evacuation, and resumed soon after the crews received the "all clear" sign. Even so, by the time the last

---

142. Mary Crouch, "Texas Baptist Men offer clean-up service and meals to flood victims," https://www.baptiststandard.com/resources/archives/44-2004-archives/2052-texas-baptist-men-offer-clean-up-service-and-meals-to-flood-victims61404.

143. John Hall, "Floods prompt outpouring of ministry," Aug. 6, 2004, https://www.baptiststandard.com/resources/archives/44-2004-archives/2298-floods-prompt-outpouring-of-ministry80904.

144. John Hall, "Texas Baptist Men teams race to work between Florida storms," Sept. 10, 2004, https://www.baptiststandard.com/resources/archives/44-2004-archives/2449-texas-baptist-men-teams-race-to-work-between-florida-storms92004.

out-of-state food-service vehicle left the Southeast in mid-October, Southern Baptists had prepared more than 3 million meals, and Baptists from Florida and Alabama were prepared to provide a continued response as needed.[145]

While some TBM disaster relief volunteers ministered in Alabama and Florida, others journeyed to Grenada, where Hurricane Ivan damaged or destroyed 90 percent of the island nation's buildings. TBM delivered donated hygiene items, sleeping bags, pots, pans, nonperishable food, chainsaws, generators and communications equipment to enable the people of Grenada to repair, rebuild and "become part of their own recovery," said Bob Dixon, who coordinated the collection of donated items throughout Texas. TBM crews set up turkey fryers at 10 churches across the country, teaching local people how to operate them. Trained TBM personnel also assisted with damage assessment and medical relief, and Victim Relief Ministries chaplains offered spiritual counsel.[146] The TBM set the stage for more international ministry that soon followed.

Christmas 2004 Tsunami

The day after Christmas 2004 brought an unwelcome present to South Asia. Early that morning, a series of earthquakes in the Indian Ocean spawned a tsunami that affected more than a dozen countries and became one of the deadliest natural disasters in recorded history, killing about a quarter-million people and prompting a worldwide humanitarian response. David Beckett, a member of Currey Creek Baptist Church in Boerne who served as a missionary in Sri Lanka with Gospel for Asia, contacted TBM and appealed for help. TBM immediately began making plans to send water purification units with trained operators to Sri Lanka, along with components to build another eight units on-site, along with food-service teams to Sri Lanka, Thailand and a refugee camp in Sumatra. Children's Emergency Relief International—an agency of Baptist Child & Family Services—was invited to set up child-care centers and establish foster care programs in Sri Lanka, and Buckner International made its inventory of shoes and socks available to ministry partners in South Asia, including the Baptist World Alliance and the Cooperative Baptist Fellowship.[147]

---

145. John Hall, "Texas Baptist Men hope disastrous season is winding down," Oct. 14, 2004, https://www.baptiststandard.com/resources/archives/44-2004-archives/2620-texas-baptist-men-hope-disastrous-season-is-winding-down101804.

146. John Hall, TBM continues serving in wake of Ivan; Grenada requests assistance, Sept. 20, 2004, https://www.baptiststandard.com/resources/archives/44-2004-archives/2507-tbm-continues-serving-in-wake-of-ivan-grenada-requests-assistance92004.

147. Ken Camp, "Texas Baptists join worldwide Tsunami relief response," Jan. 10, 2005, https://www.baptiststandard.com/resources/archives/45-2005-archives/2983-texas-baptists-join-worldwide-tsunami-relief-response11005.

Once trained TBM volunteers were on the ground in Sri Lanka with 10 water purification units, God arranged "divine appointments" to enable them to accomplish his work, noted Beckett, who eventually was named director of Sri Lanka ministry for CERI. A Canadian helped TBM officials make connections with the water board of Batticaloa in eastern Sri Lanka. "We took key leaders to the water department and told them: 'We are here to help you. We want to do what you need, not what we think you need,'" Dick Talley recalled later.[148] They discovered the municipal chlorination system needed to be repaired, wells needed to be tested to determine whether they had become contaminated when the area was inundated with saltwater, and polluted wells needed to be cleaned. At a restaurant, members of the TBM team ran into an engineer with roots both in New Zealand and Alaska. They struck up a conversation and explained what they needed to do to help local authorities. Together with the engineer, they developed a plan to clean wells. Of several proposals considered, it was only one the government ultimately approved. TBM crews went to work, cleaning anywhere from two-dozen to 30 wells a day, all the while teaching Sri Lankans how to do the work themselves. TBM volunteers also served meals to several thousand people daily and repaired water pumps and chlorination systems both for Batticaloa and Kalmunai—equipment that supplied clean water for up to 150,000 people along Sri Lanka's eastern coast.[149]

As the work in Sri Lanka continued, TBM volunteers partnered with local churches. They provided pastors with pumps and tractors to maintain the wells, improve the lives of people in their communities and share the gospel. TBM also taught the local people how to provide shelter for themselves. The Texans built simple model metal frames for houses that could be duplicated across the island, and they taught Sri Lankans how to weld them together. In the short term, residents were able to provide temporary shelter for their families by covering the frames with tarps. In the months that followed, they used cinder blocks or other sturdy materials to build permanent walls for their homes. Throughout the process, TBM volunteers taught residents skills they could use later, and they boosted the local economy by purchasing the supplies they needed in Sri Lanka.[150]

148. Interview with Dick Talley, Dallas, June 12, 2015.
149. John Hall, "TBM volunteers offer relief in Sri Lanka," Jan. 21, 2005, https://www.baptiststandard.com/resources/archives/45-2005-archives/3092-tbm-volunteers-offer-relief-in-sri-lanka12405.
150. John Hall, "Baptist relief focuses on new homes, pure water," Feb. 4, 2005, https://www.baptiststandard.com/resources/archives/45-2005-archives/3141-baptist-relief-focuses-on-new-homes-pure-water20705.

In four months, about 150 TBM volunteers served in Sri Lanka, building homes, cleaning wells and assisting at Batticaloa General Hospital. At the hospital, they purchased commercial-grade laundry equipment to help provide clean linens for patients, supplied a television, DVD player and Veggie Tales disks so children would watch Christian entertainment, and they provided care for children. They also provided a refrigerator and freezer for a temporary home for orphans and donated kitchen equipment to refugee camps, while training the people there how to use it, and also constructed a community center at a refugee camp. All the while, as they demonstrated the love of Christ by their actions, they looked for opportunities to share their faith verbally. Carroll Prewitt of Lindale, who served as an on-site coordinator for TBM in Sri Lanka, noted at least nine people professed faith in Christ while the TBM volunteers served in Vaddavaan. Five locals who served as drivers and interpreters for the TBM volunteers became Christians, as well as one member of a nongovernmental organization. Rather than discouraging the Texans' evangelistic efforts, Sri Lankan officials praised TBM for continuing to serve long after other agencies left their country. "I really think the spiritual impact is greater than anything else we're doing," Prewitt said.[151]

Tsunami relief and recovery touched the hearts and captured the imaginations of people worldwide. Children at First Baptist Church in Argyle organized a bake sale to raise money for TBM disaster relief in Sri Lanka. The small group of children created signs to advertise the sale and did much of the baking themselves. Pastor Bryan Hutchison brought his daughters—Peyton, age 9, and Madison, age 5—to Dallas to deliver to TBM Executive Director Leo Smith the more than $1,000 the church's children raised. "It's amazing what five kids can do when they put their hearts in it," Hutchison said.[152] At Park Cities Baptist Church in Dallas, Royal Ambassadors collected more than $8,700 for TBM disaster relief ministries in South Asia. The boys enlisted friends and family members to pledge amounts for each goal they could make in a basketball-shooting event. The RAs shot baskets for three hours one night, and in the process, they nearly tripled their previous record for annual disaster relief giving. Smith presented a Sri Lankan flag to the RA

---

151. John Hall, "TBM building new lives in Sri Lanka," March 17, 2005, https://www. baptiststandard.com/resources/archives/45-2005-archives/3320-tbm-building-new-lives-in-sri-lanka32105.

152. John Hall, "Argyle children offer sweet relief," March 4, 2005, https://www. baptiststandard.com/resources/archives/45-2005-archives/3254-argyle-children-offer-sweet-relief30705.

---

chapter, asking the boys and their leaders to pray for the people of Sri Lanka every time they looked at it.[153]

Deadly sisters, Katrina and Rita

On Aug. 29, 2005, Hurricane Katrina made landfall in southeastern Louisiana with sustained winds of 125 mph, and it maintained much of its intensity as it moved into Mississippi. One day earlier, New Orleans Mayor Ray Nagin had ordered the first-ever mandatory evacuation of his city. Thousands who lacked transportation or financial means to leave the city were sheltered at the Louisiana Superdome several days. Thousands of others remained in their homes, and many lost their lives when floodwaters breached the city's levees at dozens of points. By the time Katrina's fury was spent, she claimed about 2,000 lives in multiple states, affected about 90,000 square miles and caused more than $100 billion in property damage.

When Louisiana residents began their evacuation, Texas Baptist churches opened their doors as shelters. About 400 people filled the facilities at North Orange Baptist Church, including one woman who went into labor at the shelter and had to be rushed to a hospital, and another 115 found shelter in the gymnasium at First Baptist Church in Orange. Memorial Baptist Church in Baytown provided shelter for about 250 people, and more than 100 moved into the Shepherd's Inn community ministry center in Port Arthur.[154]

Immediately after the hurricane hit, TBM mobilized disaster relief volunteers. After staging in Marshall, the teams moved into Louisiana. The statewide emergency food-service unit, the mobile command center and a shower unit from the Hill Country traveled to Lafayette, and the Top O' Texas food-service crew went to Alexandria. Disaster relief units from Tarrant, Dallas and Permian Basin Baptist associations were sent to Hammond. Meanwhile, the South Texas food-service team was dispatched to Orange, to assist in ministry to evacuees.[155] Later, crews were deployed to Covington, La., and Biloxi, Miss., as well as to an evacuation site in San Antonio. Within two weeks, TBM emergency food-service crews prepared more than a half-million meals in Mississippi, Louisiana and Texas.[156]

153. John Hall, "Tsunami looks different through a child's eyes," April 1, 2005, https://www.baptiststandard.com/resources/archives/45-2005-archives/3376-tsunami-looks-different-through-childs-eyes40405.

154. John Hall, "Baptists respond in wake of Hurricane Katrina's fury," Sept. 2, 2005, https://www.baptiststandard.com/resources/archives/45-2005-archives/4004-baptists-respond-in-wake-of-hurricane-katrinas-fury.

155. *Ibid.*

156. John Hall, "TBM serves more than 500,000 meals," Sept. 16, 2005, https://www.baptiststandard.com/resources/archives/45-2005-archives/4097-tbm-serves-more-than-500000-meals.

At the same time Texas Baptist churches and Baptist encampments continued to shelter Katrina evacuees and TBM moved from emergency food-service to mud-out operations in Louisiana, Texas braced for the impact of another storm. On Sept. 21, Hurricane Rita achieved Category 5 status. Before it made landfall near Sabine Pass three days later, it weakened to a Category 3 hurricane, but it still packed 120 mph winds. TBM mobilized volunteers, staging the food-service team from Permian Basin, the shower unit from the Hill Country and the laundry unit from Austin at Latham Springs Baptist Encampment, near Aquilla. The statewide and East Texas food-service units and crews from Dallas and Bluebonnet Baptist Association traveled to San Antonio in preparation, as more than 2.5 million people from coastal communities evacuated. By the end of September, TBM food-service volunteers were stationed in San Antonio, Nacogdoches, Newton, Orange, Center, Beaumont, Corrigan and Wichita Falls.[157]

The crew that set up operations at Beaumont's Ford Center cooked more than 8,000 meals a day, particularly serving first-responders. The team first staged in Beaumont, then was directed to Huntsville, redirected to Houston and finally steered to Beaumont. In spite of the challenges, the team members never lost sight of whom they were representing. "Every one of these guys has a heart for Jesus," said Larry Burks, the team's coordinator. "They love him. They know if he were here walking the Earth, he'd be helping people. We're his ambassadors, so to speak."[158]

157. "Texas Baptist Men provide disaster relief," Sept. 30, 2005, https://www. baptiststandard.com/resources/archives/45-2005-archives/4154-texas-baptist-men-provide-disaster-relief.

158. John Hall, "TBM cooking 8,000 meals a day in Beaumont," Oct. 3, 2005, https://www. baptiststandard.com/resources/archives/45-2005-archives/4169-tbm-cooking-8000-meals-a-day-in-beaumont.

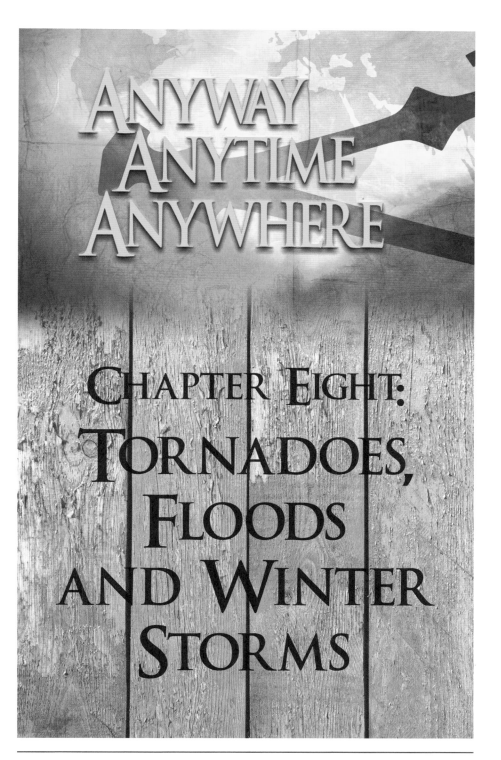

CHAPTER EIGHT:

TORNADOES, FLOODS AND WINTER STORMS

CHAPTER EIGHT: TORNADOES, FLOODS AND WINTER STORMS

After some of the most destructive hurricanes in United States history and a South Asian tsunami branded as one of the most devastating natural disasters in recorded history, Texas Baptist Men disaster relief volunteers entered into a couple of years of more routine ministry. Of course, no disaster is routine for the people whose lives it disrupts, nor is any disaster relief exercise identical to any other. So, TBM spent much of 2006 and 2007

Coordination of disaster relief operations demands careful planning, logistical know-how and plenty of coffee.

responding to a series of uniquely typical and routinely distinctive disasters generally closer to home, as well as providing disaster relief training to ministry partners in Brazil and Mexico.

Twisting winds and rising water

On May 9, 2006, a pair of F3 tornadoes swept through northeastern Collin County, claiming three lives and damaging more than two-dozen homes. Westminster was hit particularly hard, and TBM focused its ministry primarily on that community. TBM volunteers went door-to-door through the town of about 400 residents, offering help to families who needed their services. Chainsaw crews helped clear downed trees and other debris. Other TBM volunteers helped residents with roof damage by covering their homes with blue tarps as a temporary shelter. Others just needed someone to listen to their stories, and TBM volunteers and Victim Relief Ministries chaplains listened to them, offered words of encouragement and prayed with them.[159]

In late July, thunderstorms hit the westernmost parts of Texas. El Paso received twice its average amount of rainfall within a matter of days. Floodwaters damaged more than 1,200 homes and destroyed nearly 300. When the waters began to recede, TBM volunteers moved in to help. Mud-out and clean-out crews from around the state focused primarily on the southern and western parts of the city, removing damaged furniture from homes, ripping out soaked carpet and spongy sheetrock, pressure-washing surfaces and disinfecting homes to prevent mold and mildew.

Mary Bess Jackson from First Baptist Church in Midlothian served with one of those teams, and she recalled encountering families who did not know where to turn after the water swept away most of their belongings. "Those people need a hope and a future," she said, as a tear stained her cheek. "And God can give it to them through Christ."[160]

Rey Villanueva from Choate Baptist Church near Kenedy recalled a man he encountered who had lost nearly everything he owned. All he could think about was the destruction, the devastation and the loss. TBM volunteers worked patiently with him, helping him sort through possessions in his home and waiting as he decided what to keep and what to discard. Throughout the experience, they listened as he poured out his heart. Before the crew left, the homeowner prayed with the volunteers. Villanueva recalled how the same man who had been unable to think beyond the pain of his recent past began to envision a future for himself and his family. "It was just a complete transformation by the time we left," he said.[161]

Crippling winter storms in the Midwest

In mid-January, 2007, freezing rain, sleet and ice covered Oklahoma, prompting Gov. Brad Henry to declare a state of emergency. McAlester, in eastern Oklahoma, lost all electrical power for an extended period, and thousands of residents moved into shelters, including a major one at First Baptist Church. Three-dozen TBM chainsaw volunteers from Harmony-Pittsburg and Collin Baptist associations, Lake Pointe Church in Rockwall

---

159. John Hall, "Baptists help after tornado," May 12, 2006, https://www.baptiststandard.com/resources/archives/46-2006-archives/5045-baptists-help-after-tornado.

160. John Hall, "TBM helps flood victims in El Paso, Aug. 18, 2006, https://www.baptiststandard.com/resources/archives/46-2006-archives/5418-tbm-helps-flood-victims-in-el-paso.

161. *Ibid.*

and Paramount Baptist Church in Amarillo braved icy roads to make the hazardous trek to McAlester.[162] Within two weeks, about 100 TBM volunteers were serving in McAlester and Pryor. David Harrison, former fire chief in Pryor, called it the worst ice storm he had seen in 29 years. A TBM food-service crew set up in Grove, north of Pryor, where they prepared more than 10,000 meals in a short time. Chainsaw crews encountered unfamiliar conditions, putting into practice techniques most had never been called on to use before as they worked on ice-covered trees and were pelted with sleet. "My team does a lot of climbing. When you start climbing a tree with ice, it's a lot more difficult," TBM disaster relief team leader Joe Detterman of Collin Baptist Association said. "The wood is brittle, and it breaks when you don't expect it or when you don't want it to." Even so, the volunteers put themselves in challenging places for one reason, he stressed. "We do this for one purpose, and that's to share the love of God."[163]

In the weeks that followed, TBM crews expanded their ministry to provide disaster relief to ice storm survivors in southwestern Missouri. Three chainsaw crews from Texas worked in an area about 70 miles southwest of Springfield, Mo., responding to a request from the Southern Baptist Convention's North American Mission Board. They were among 15 teams from 17 states—about 1,000 volunteers—who responded to NAMB's request for help. TBM volunteers also transported a generator to a fire station in Seneca, Mo., to create a "warming station" for elderly residents, as well as first-responders. By early March, NAMB reported Baptist volunteers had prepared more than 100,000 meals and completed at least 3,300 chainsaw jobs, as well as washing hundreds of loads of laundry and providing access to showers. In the process, they recorded 33 professions of faith in Christ.[164]

Widespread spring storms

The arrival of spring spelled the end of ice storms but marked the beginning of a series of thunderstorms and tornadoes throughout Texas, as well as across the border in northern Mexico. A mid-April tornado damaged more than 150 homes and claimed two lives in Tarrant County. Storms left two

162. Barbara Bedrick, "TBM chainsaw teams serve in Oklahoma," Jan. 19, 2007, https://www.baptiststandard.com/resources/archives/47-2007-archives/6064-tbm-chainsaw-teams-serve-in-oklahoma.

163. Barbara Bedrick, "TBM chainsaw teams offer relief in northeastern Oklahoma," Feb. 2, 2007, https://www.baptiststandard.com/resources/archives/47-2007-archives/6088-tbm-chainsaw-teams-offer-relief-in-northeastern-oklahoma.

164. Barbara Bedrick, "Texas Baptists aid Missouri families," March 2, 2007, https://www.baptiststandard.com/resources/archives/47-2007-archives/6176-texas-baptists-aid-missouri-families.

church buildings in shambles and tore the roofs off multiple homes in Haltom City. Tree limbs five feet in circumference pierced the roof of Ruth Gunson's home, while she and her family found shelter under a mattress during the worst of the storm. "We have no electricity and no insurance, but we're alive," she said several days later.[165] Texas Baptist Men disaster relief volunteers spent hours on her rooftop, working to remove the limbs and to cover the damaged roof temporarily. Victim Relief Ministries chaplains served alongside them, helping with clean-up efforts, praying with the family and bringing them pizza.

Little more than a week after the tornado hit Tarrant County, a storm swept through the Texas Panhandle. In Cactus, a town of about 3,000 people an hour north of Amarillo, a tornado destroyed the community's water tower and destroyed about one-third of the town. About 140 miles to the south, James Hassell, then pastor of First Baptist Church in Tulia, was visiting his neighbor—a Methodist minister—when the tornado hit. The funnel cloud spread debris in all directions but missed First Baptist Church by just a few blocks. TBM mobilized volunteers with the Top O'Texas Baptist Association food-service unit, a chainsaw team from Paramount Baptist Church in Amarillo, a mobile shower unit from O'Donnell and a childcare unit to respond to needs in Tulia and Cactus. After Cactus lost electricity, tornado survivors found shelter 10 miles away in Dumas, where TBM set up a field kitchen adjacent to the Moore County Community Center and served more than 1,500 meals a day. In Tulia, TBM volunteers worked in the kitchen at First Baptist Church alongside members of the congregation, cooking and serving meals. When inmates from nearby prisons were employed to assist with the clean-up effort, First Baptist in Tulia provided their evening meals.[166]

On April 24, a tornado hit Piedras Negras and Eagle Pass, border towns on either side of the Rio Grande, killing at least 10 people, injuring more than 70 and destroying 20 homes, particularly in one devastated eight-block-wide area. "It looked like a bomb exploded," said Robert Cepeda, church starter with the Baptist General Convention of Texas.[167] TBM responded swiftly, sending a food-service team from Permian Basin Baptist Association, along with chainsaw volunteers, damage assessors, a mobile shower unit and

---

165. Barbara Bedrick, "Volunteers provide relief when tornado hits North Texas," April 16, 2007, https://www.baptiststandard.com/resources/archives/47-2007-archives/6383-volunteers-provide-relief-when-tornado-hits-north-texas.

166. Barbara Bedrick, "Texas Baptists offer relief to victims of widespread storms," April 27, 2007, https://www.baptiststandard.com/resources/archives/47-2007-archives/6414-texas-baptists-offer-relief-to-victims-of-widespread-storms.

167. *Ibid.*

clean-up teams. In Piedras Negras, TBM volunteers worked in the shadow of the remnants of a 200-year-old Catholic church, cooking 4,500 meals a day for survivors and recovery workers. "We're an extension of the local Baptist church," TBM Ethnic Coordinator Ed Alvarado said. "We're hoping our presence will influence and undergird the local churches in Piedras Negras."[168]

Growing out of Texas Baptist ministry along the Rio Grande, TBM's history of disaster relief in Mexico and a partnership between Texas Baptists and Mexico, TBM received an invitation to train top-ranking Mexican governmental officials in disaster response. Working with three Baptist churches in Juarez, Alvarado and Gary Smith of Dallas led the three-day training event for Mexican officials, pastors and church leaders. Previously, a similar partnership had opened the door to TBM and the Baptist General Convention of Texas helping set up a similar program in Brazil. Dexton Shores, director of BGCT missions in Mexico and along the Rio Grande, helped TBM volunteers deliver more than 250 ceramic water filters to pastors and others in Mexico. In addition to providing much-needed training about disaster relief, the partnership also boosted the standing of Juarez pastors by validating their ministry and elevating them in the eyes of political officials, BGCT Missions Team Leader Josué Valerio said. "The government is acknowledging the Baptist ministry in its city," he said. "This opens the door for a greater ministry and lifts up the name of Christ."[169]

Rising floods, consistent ministry

A series of unseasonable floods in summer 2007 prompted a widespread TBM response. Along the Red River, rising water swamped about 500 homes in the Gainesville area and claimed five lives. Almost immediately, local Baptists provided meals for displaced residents. Soon, TBM joined them, serving more than 500 meals a day and cleaning mud and debris from damaged homes in late June.[170] In two weeks, volunteers with the Wichita-Archer-Clay Baptist Association food-service unit provided about 14,000 meals. Over the July 4 holiday, a half-dozen TBM crews worked to restore

168. John Hall, "Texas Baptists minister in Piedras Negras," May 11, 2007, https://www.baptiststandard.com/resources/archives/47-2007-archives/6429-texas-baptists-minister-in-piedras-negras.

169. Barbara Bedrick, "TBM trains Mexico's top-ranking officials in disaster response," May 29, 2007, https://www.baptiststandard.com/resources/archives/47-2007-archives/6538-tbm-trains-mexicos-top-ranking-officials-in-disaster-response.

170. John Hall, "Baptists throw a lifeline to flooded Gainesville," June 22, 2007, https://www.baptiststandard.com/resources/archives/47-2007-archives/6627-baptists-throw-a-lifeline-to-flooded-gainesville.

homes and bring hope to several North Texas communities. A mobile shower unit from Park Cities Baptist Church in Dallas set up at Allendale Baptist Church in Wichita Falls, where volunteer crews were lodged. Mud-out and clean-up crews from Collin Baptist Association completed about two-dozen jobs. The mobile shower and laundry unit from Lamesa Baptist Association provided access to 386 showers and washed 367 loads of laundry, and volunteers with the state childcare unit cared for more than 70 children. A half-hour to the east in Sherman, crews from Lubbock Baptist Association and Paramount Baptist Church in Amarillo helped residents recover from storm damage. Also in North Texas, the Tarrant Baptist Association food-service unit provided more than 800 meals to storm victims in Haltom City. Meanwhile, when downed trees and broken limbs clogged already rain-swollen creeks in the Marble Falls area of Central Texas, a chainsaw crew from Burnet-Llano Baptist Association went to work clearing away the debris. TBM volunteers from Second Baptist Church in LaGrange responded to needs in Copperas Cove, where a tornado and rising water displaced families. The LaGrange crew helped six families clear out flood-damaged homes, and blue-tarp roofers and chainsaw crews from the Killeen/Fort Hood area worked in the same area.[171]

When the Seco River flooded homes in D'Hanis, TBM volunteers responded to an invitation from First Baptist Church in Hondo to help families in the area. A clean-out crew from Second Baptist Church in LaGrange and the shower and laundry unit from Austin Baptist Association assisted members of the congregation in ministering to their neighbors. "People are hurting," said Ross Chandler, pastor of First Baptist Church in Hondo. "We are trying to meet those needs, because it's what Jesus would do."[172]

When Hurricane Humberto made landfall in Southeast Texas in mid-September, dumping up to 16 inches of rain on the region and leaving more than 110,000 people without electricity, TBM sent in an emergency food-service team to work in Vidor, Orange and Winnie. At the same time, TBM volunteers responded to a request from missionaries Jim and Viola Palmer for help significantly farther away. Twelve chainsaw crews journeyed to Nicaragua to help in the wake of Hurricane Felix, a Category 5 storm that hit the nation with winds as strong as 155 miles per hour. The storm "knocked

---

171. Barbara Bedrick, "No holiday for Texas Baptist disaster relief workers," July 6, 2007, https://www.baptiststandard.com/resources/archives/47-2007-archives/6697-no-holiday-for-texas-baptist-disaster-relief-workers.

172. Jessica Dooley, "Baptist volunteers rebuilding lives one house at a time," Aug. 3, 2007, https://www.baptiststandard.com/resources/archives/47-2007-archives/6794-baptist-volunteers-rebuilding-lives-one-house-at-a-time.

down pretty much every tree" on a five-acre experimental farm operated by the Baptist mission in Nicaragua, Palmer noted. The mission house where the Palmers lived lost its roof and a "good portion" of the second floor, he added. It marked the third hurricane the Palmers lived through during their time as International Mission Board missionaries in Nicaragua.[173]

Two months later, TBM mobilized disaster relief volunteers to serve in southern Mexico after more than a week of heavy rain caused the Grijalva River to burst its banks, flooding 70 percent of the state of Tabasco, displacing up to 800,000 people and causing lethal mudslides. TBM activated its South Texas disaster relief unit, transported two water purifiers to the region and enlisted emergency food-service workers to serve through Thanksgiving. "Because of the heavy rains and the flood, the people have lost all their belongings—houses, vehicles, food, clothes and personal items," said C.P. Raul Catellanos Fernandez, chief executive officer of the National Baptist Convention of Mexico.[174] While a TBM crew was traveling to Tabasco, tragedy struck. A group of children surrounded the TBM team's van while it made its way through a small Mexican village. As the children darted around the slow-moving vehicle in an attempt to sell items to passengers, one child was hit. A volunteer trained in emergency medical procedures examined the child and noticed a gash on the boy's head, but he reported the child's vital signs were strong. An ambulance rushed the boy to a nearby hospital for treatment. Later, he was transferred to another hospital where he died two days after the accident. Local authorities detained the van's driver, but they soon released him and cleared him of all charges.[175]

173. John Hall and Ferrell Foster, "Texas Baptist Men feeding units called out to aid hurricane victims," Sept. 14, 2007, https://www.baptiststandard.com/resources/archives/47-2007-archives/6954-texas-baptist-men-feeding-units-called-to-aid-hurricane-victims.

174. Ken Camp, "TBM mobilizes disaster relief team to meet needs in southern Mexico," Nov. 15, 2007, https://www.baptiststandard.com/resources/archives/47-2007-archives/7189-tbm-mobilizes-disaster-relief-team-to-meet-needs-in-southern-mexico.

175. John Hall, "Child dies following accident involving TBM volunteers in Mexico," Nov. 19, 2007, https://www.baptiststandard.com/resources/archives/47-2007-archives/7236-child-killed-following-accident-involving-tbm-volunteers-in-mexico.

ANYWAY ANYTIME ANYWHERE

CHAPTER NINE:
SPECIAL NEEDS, SPECIAL MINISTRIES, SPECIAL OPPORTUNITIES

CHAPTER NINE:
SPECIAL NEEDS, SPECIAL MINISTRIES,
SPECIAL OPPORTUNITIES

Volunteers work behind the scenes at the Dixon Missions Equipping Center in Dallas to help disaster relief operations run smoothly.

If 2006-07 marked a time of routine disaster relief, the kind of ministry for which volunteers train and directors prepare, 2008 represented a period of response to special needs that demanded creative and specialized ministries. Sometimes, this meant adapting to varied contexts and locales. Sometimes, it meant flexibility in answering to God's call to minister on the far side of the world. Sometimes, it meant responding to back-to-back or simultaneous disasters across vast stretches of Texas.

Caring for children from a polygamist sect

On April 3-4, Texas Child Protective Services and law enforcement officials entered a compound near Eldorado built by Warren Jeffs of the polygamist Fundamentalist Church of Jesus Christ of Latter-day Saints. In response to allegations of widespread abuse, state investigators and law officers removed 416 children and 139 women from the 1,619-acre Yearning for Zion Ranch. First Baptist Church in Eldorado immediately opened its facilities to house up to 80 of the women and children temporarily and made two church buses available to state agencies to aid in their removal from the rural compound. The West Texas director for Buckner Children and Family Services worked as a consultant and first responder throughout the relocation.

Within a few days, the women and children were moved to a multi-site shelter in San Angelo, where San Antonio-based Baptist Child & Family Services took a lead role at the request of the Governor's Division of Emergency Management. Within a few days after the Yearning for Zion Ranch raid, seven shelters were operating on the grounds of historic Fort Concho, and 50 BCFS staff worked on-site. TBM made available portable shower and laundry units for the shelters, and emergency food-service teams prepared meals. BCFS personnel and TBM volunteers soon learned about the unique needs of the women and children. Mothers prohibited their children from playing with certain toys. Adherents found the color red objectionable because they attached theological significance to it. Most pertinent to the TBM crews, the sheltered population only ate organic, non-processed food. So, the teams learned to adapt their menus—a task they also were called upon to do when serving evacuees from nursing homes after a natural disaster. So, the San Angelo food-service team became specialty unit, focusing on cooking for groups with special dietary needs.[176]

Bound for Burma, Training in Thailand

On May 2, Cyclone Nargis struck Myanmar, also known historically as Burma. Early official estimates were 23,000 deaths and 42,000 missing. Eventually, the numbers swelled to 84,500 dead and 53,800 missing. The United Nations estimated 2.4 million people were affected by the disaster.[177] Nine days after the storm made landfall, TBM sent a seven-member rapid-response team to Bangkok, Thailand, in response to a request submitted by Saddleback Church in Lake Forest, Calif., and The Fellowship of The Woodlands near Houston. Team members hoped to enter Myanmar to assess needs and explore opportunities for follow-up teams to meet needs in the country. [178]

Once the TBM team arrived in Bangkok, their mission gained a new focus. Members of Baptist World Aid's Rescue 24 search, rescue and relief team, led by Hungarian Baptist Aid, were granted visas to enter Myanmar to assess needs. So, instead of duplicating efforts and seeking entry into the restricted

176. Ken Camp, "Texas Baptists minister in wake of raid on polygamist compound," April 10, 2008, https://www.baptiststandard.com/resources/archives/48-2008-archives/7747-texas-baptists-minister-in-wake-of-raid-on-polygamist-compound.

177. "Myanmar: Cyclone Nargis 2008 Facts and Figures," International Federation of Red Cross and Red Crescent Societies, http://www.ifrc.org/en/news-and-media/news-stories/asia-pacific/myanmar/myanmar-cyclone-nargis-2008-facts-and-figures/.

178. John Hall, "TBM responds to Myanmar cyclone," May 13, 2008, https://www.baptiststandard.com/resources/archives/48-2008-archives/7880-tbm-responds-to-myanmar-cyclone.

country to meet needs directly, TBM volunteers determined they could serve most effectively by operating a training base for Burmese Christians in Thailand. "We try to go wherever doors open and see how we can minister to people in need," TBM Associate Executive Director Mickey Lenamon said.[179]

Two months later at a Renewing Your Passion missions conference in Dallas, a Gospel for Asia representative from Myanmar described conditions in his country. Prior to the cyclone, more than 150,000 Burmese were housed in refugee camps along the border of Myanmar and China. Poverty dropped the Burmese life expectancy to 56 years, compared to 71 years in neighboring Thailand. The cyclone made life even more unbearable, when 1.3 million acres of fertile cropland was damaged. Gospel for Asia teams delivered emergency food and supplies into Myanmar after the disaster. Two Buddhist families who went without food two weeks after the storm later told the team: "Buddha did nothing while we were suffering, but your Jesus loves us."[180]

Doing what Jesus asked

In early June, heavy rains swept through the Midwest. Unusually heavy winter snow already had rivers running at exceptionally high levels and left the ground saturated. So, when the early summer rain began, it resulted in a flood of historic proportions, devastating the Cedar Rapids, Iowa City, Oakville and Gulfport areas.[181] In a short time, floodwaters inundated 1,300 city blocks in Cedar Rapids, displacing more than 26,000 people. TBM units with 71 volunteers responded to the need at the request of the Southern Baptist Convention's North American Mission Board. A food-service team from First Baptist Church in Plains set up a field kitchen at Immanuel Baptist Church in Cedar Rapids and prepared 3,200 hot meals for the American Red Cross to deliver on June 17, the first day officials allowed residents to return to some neighborhoods.[182] They were joined by a shower unit from Lamesa. In the weeks that followed, several TBM mud-out crews made the

179. "TBM team to train Burmese in Thailand," May 18, 2008, https://www.baptiststandard.com/news/texas/7889-tbm-team-to-train-burmese-in-thailand.

180. "Myanmar Christian tells conference how God is changing lives after cyclone disaster," July 12, 2008, https://www.baptiststandard.com/news/texas/8248-myanmar-christian-tells-conference-how-god-is-changing-lives-after-cyclone-disaster.

181. "Meteorological Factors Leading up to the Flood of 2008," National Weather Service, https://www.weather.gov/dvn/flood2008_Overview.

182. Kaitlin Chapman, "Texas Baptist Men offer relief to Iowa flood victims," June 17, 2008, https://www.baptiststandard.com/news/texas/8127-texas-baptist-men-offer-relief-to-iowa-flood-victims.

1,000-plus-mile journey to Iowa. "Jesus loves us, and we come up here as a testimony of that love and to help people devastated by the floods," said Gerry Jones, a volunteer on the state disaster relief mobile unit. "We are just doing what Jesus has asked us to do." [183]

A few weeks later, "doing what Jesus has asked" involved responding to devastation Hurricane Dolly caused in the Rio Grande Valley. In the wake of the Category 2 hurricane, a TBM crew from San Antonio was dispatched to McAllen to support a shelter for people with special needs, a Dallas-based crew traveled to Harlingen, and an East Texas team worked in Brownsville.[184] After the devastation caused by Hurricane Rita and Hurricane Katrina in 2005—and the around-the-clock news coverage that followed—people whose lives were disrupted by Hurricane Dolly found themselves victims of compassion fatigue. "Because of the diminished magnitude, people have not sensed the need to respond," Gary Smith, volunteer disaster relief coordinator from Dallas, told a reporter at the time. "The needs of the people are as urgent as they were in Rita and Katrina. Texas Baptist Men is in the Valley offering a cold cup of water in Jesus' name."[185] By the time TBM completed its food-service ministry in South Texas Aug. 5, crews prepared more than 375,000 meals, and recovery volunteers continued to remove debris and damaged walls from homes and help survivors sort through and store their possessions.[186]

In late August, TBM state disaster relief directors placed all volunteers on alert in anticipation of Hurricane Gustav, which had hit Haiti, Jamaica and Cuba. TBM mobilized food-service teams as people began to evacuate southern Louisiana, and many were expected to seek shelter in East Texas. San Antonio-based Baptist Child & Family Services sheltered evacuees with special needs. Nationally, more than 100 Southern Baptist food-service units were placed on alert.[187] "It's like we're waiting for the shoe to fall," Smith told a Texas Baptist reporter at the time.[188] Although Gustav did not cause

---

183. *Ibid.*

184. "Update: TBM activates feeding units," July 22, 2008, https://www.baptiststandard. com/news/texas/8299-update-tbm-activates-feeding-units.

185. "Texas Baptists offer helping hand after Dolly," July 29, 2008, https://www. baptiststandard.com/news/texas/8322-texas-baptists-offer-helping-hand-after-dolly.

186. John Hall, "Texas Baptist disaster relief shifts to recovery in Valley," Aug. 6, 2008, https://www.baptiststandard.com/news/texas/8367-texas-baptist-disaster-relief-shifts-to-recovery-in-valley.

187. "Texas Baptist ministries gear up for Hurricane Gustav," Aug. 29, 2008, https://www. baptiststandard.com/news/texas/8469-texas-baptist-ministries-gear-up-for-hurricane-gustav.

188. John Hall, "Texas Baptist Men feed evacuees; BCFS shelters people with special needs," https://www.baptiststandard.com/news/texas/8470-texas-baptist-men-feed-evacuees-bcfs-shelters-people-with-special-needs.

the level of disruption in Texas some prognosticators predicted, TBM did prepare about 25,000 meals for evacuees who found shelter in Bryan, Lufkin, Marshall and Lufkin. The experience also provided a warm-up exercise for another hurricane that soon followed.

Hurricane Ike

On Sept. 4, Hurricane Ike reached Category 4 status in the Atlantic Ocean before hitting Cuba four days later. Although it initially weakened, it regained intensity as it tracked westward through the Gulf of Mexico. President George W. Bush declared a state of emergency along the Texas Gulf Coast, and South Texas prepared for the storm's onslaught. South Texas Children's Home closed its Corpus Christi campus, and Buckner International evacuated retirement and children's facilities in Beaumont. Baptist Child & Family Services opened shelters in San Antonio for evacuees with special needs with the cooperation of at least 20 churches. By Sept. 9, officials called for the evacuation of all special-needs residents in Corpus Christi, and Galveston-area authorities ordered a mandatory evacuation of all residents of one Brazoria County ZIP Code. TBM mobilized food-service and shower units.[189] Within 24 hours after Ike swept through the eastern third of the state, TBM had activated all its mobile kitchens, and officials told volunteers to prepare to serve up to 110,000 meals a day, as they set up operations in League City, Beaumont, Orange, Bryan, Marshall, The Woodlands and San Antonio.[190]

In Huntsville, TBM chainsaw crews from First Baptist Church in San Antonio and First Baptist Church in Athens worked to remove trees that had fallen on homes or blocked driveways. "It's what the Bible tells us to do," Jimmy Leatherwood of Athens said. "We love to do it. The people need it. … We like to help people. That's part of our church. … We're doing it in God's name."[191]

Hurricane Ike caused multimillion-dollar damage to the Houston Baptist University campus, but none of the 60 students and emergency personnel who sought shelter on the campus sustained any injury.[192] Classes resumed

---

189. John Hall, "Texas Baptists move into action as Ike aims for Texas coast," Sept. 9, 2008, https://www.baptiststandard.com/news/texas/8495-texas-baptists-move-into-action-as-ike-aims-for-texas-coast.

190. John Hall, "Texas Baptists respond rapidly to disaster in Southeast Texas," Sept. 14, 2008, https://www.baptiststandard.com/news/texas/8524-texas-baptists-respond-rapidly-to-disaster-in-southeast-texas.

191. John Hall, "Baptist volunteers have energy to spare and share," Sept. 17, 2008, https://www.baptiststandard.com/news/texas/8530-baptist-volunteers-have-energy-to-spare-and-share.

192. Martha Morrow, "Hurricane Ike has significant impact on HBU," Sept. 15, 2008, https://www.baptiststandard.com/news/texas/8528-hurricane-ike-has-significant-impact-on-hbu.

Sept. 22, eight days after Ike hit, and students who remained on campus in the days immediately after the storm made landfall helped their neighbors by volunteering. *"There is a definite bond among these young people, built on prayer, friendship and youthful optimism,"* HBU President Robert Sloan said.[193] Other Texas Baptist institutions and agencies sustained moderate damage, and many experienced extended power outages. East Texas Baptist University in Marshall was left without electricity 28 hours, but students volunteered at eight shelters in the area.[194] At Gracewood in Houston, a facility for single mothers with children, residents "rode out the storm, emerging to find evidence of Ike's fury all around them," said Don Cramer, vice president and chief operating officer for the Children at Heart Foundation.[195] Churches throughout Southeast Texas sustained damage including at least 20 congregations in Union Baptist Association.[196]

More than 1,500 TBM volunteers served in the immediate aftermath of Hurricane Ike. Food-service teams prepared more than 420,000 meals in about two weeks. Shower and laundry units enabled displaced residents and volunteers to take more than 3,000 showers and wash about 1,600 loads of laundry. Hundreds more participated in recovery and rebuilding efforts in the weeks and months that followed the disaster.[197] Nationally, Southern Baptist disaster relief volunteers prepared more than 2 million meals in the wake of Hurricanes Ike and Gustav. In three weeks, the Baptist volunteers from multiple states served more than 40,000 volunteer days, completed more than 1,200 chainsaw jobs, provided more than 24,500 showers, washed nearly 5,000 loads of laundry, purified at least 7,000 gallons of water and led 125 people to faith in Christ.[198]

Ministry in the Georgia Republic

An extraordinary commitment of time, energy and personnel to disaster relief close to home did not prevent TBM from responding when a call for

193. John Hall, "Wrap-up: After Ike, slow recovery process begins," Sept. 24, 2008, https://www.baptiststandard.com/news/texas/8578-wrap-up-after-ike-slow-recovery-process-begins.

194. Mike Midkiff, "Ike knocks out power at ETBU, but students serve evacuees," Sept. 21, 2008, https://www.baptiststandard.com/news/texas/8537-ike-knocks-out-power-at-etbu-but-students-serve-evacuees.

195. Hall, "Wrap-up," Sept. 24, 2008.

196. John Hall, "Hurricane Ike damages churches throughout Southeast Texas," Sept. 22, 2008, https://www.baptiststandard.com/news/texas/8544-hurricane-ike-damages-churches-throughout-southeast-texas.

197. Hall, "Wrap-up," Sept. 24, 2008.

198. "Baptist Briefs: Relief workers pass mileposts," Sept. 24, 2008, https://www.baptiststandard.com/news/baptist/8554-baptist-briefs-relief-workers-pass-mileposts.

help arrived from the other side of the world. In late August, TBM sent a seven-member disaster relief team to the Republic of Georgia to feed people affected by fighting in the Russian-occupied Eurasian nation.[199] The volunteers established a field kitchen in Gori, where they fed people who had taken refuge in 18 kindergarten buildings—some of whom had not eaten a hot meal in more than three weeks.[200] The TBM crew set up the food-service operation as Russian troops pulled back from a ridge just three miles away. They served about 14,000 meals in eight days before they turned the operation over to Baptist volunteers from Kentucky and Oklahoma.

"I think this was the best team ever put together," TBM team leader Larry Blanchard of Lindale said, noting the crew members were experienced at working in adverse circumstances. "They had all kinds of expertise and knew how to bob and weave and duck the big ones and still come out winners."[201]

The TBM team worked with local Christian volunteers from a church in Gori. "The pastor's sister-in-law become our head cook, because she could season the food to taste like the people would want it, not like we'd normally do it in Texas," Blanchard said. "By the last day, 16 women were in the kitchen, peeling potatoes and chopping carrots, onion and parsley for the next day." [202]

The Texas volunteers felt moved by the heartfelt gratitude the people of Gori expressed, sometimes without even being able to communicate verbally. "People would come to us, put their hands over their hearts and bow as their way of thanking us," Blanchard recalled. "We couldn't understand what each other said, but our hearts were in tune with theirs."[203]

199. John Hall, "TBM volunteers dispatched to Georgia Republic," Aug. 26, 2008, https://www.baptiststandard.com/news/texas/8453-tbm-volunteers-dispatched-to-georgia-republic.

200. Mark Kelly, "Texas volunteers serve 2,000 refugees in Gori," Sept. 2, 2008, https://www.baptiststandard.com/news/world/8477-texas-volunteers-serve-2000-refugees-in-gori.

201. Mark Kelly, "Texas volunteers help prepare 14,000 meals in Georgia Republic," *Baptist Standard*, Sept. 29, 2008, p. 18.

202. *Ibid.*

203. *Ibid.*

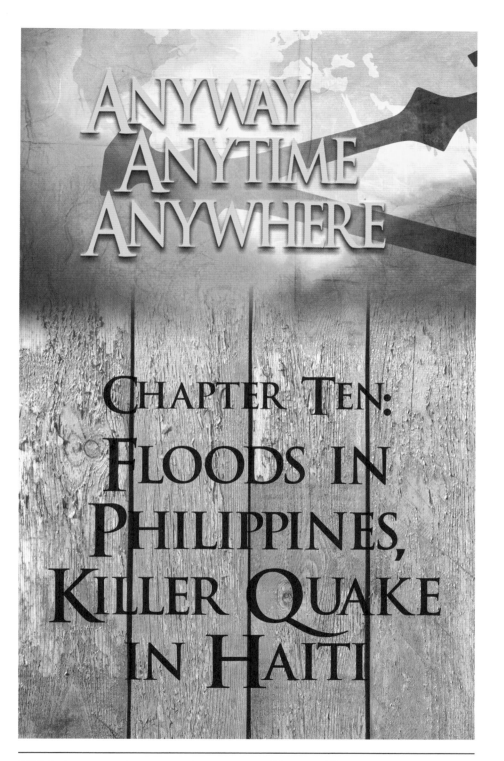

ANYWAY ANYTIME ANYWHERE

CHAPTER TEN:
FLOODS IN PHILIPPINES, KILLER QUAKE IN HAITI

CHAPTER TEN:
FLOODS IN PHILIPPINES,
KILLER QUAKE IN HAITI

The Time it Never Rained—Revisited

Some Texas Baptist Men responses to disaster involve adventures to dangerous places in far-flung locations. Some responses are prompted by appeals from heads of state or international agencies. Sometimes, the response simply requires sensitivity to the needs of neighbors and the Holy Spirit's guidance.

More than 40 years ago, Texas author Elmer Kelton wrote his novel, *The Time It Never Rained*, about the Texas drought of the 1950s and its impact on farmers and ranchers. In 2009, rural residents of Central Texas wondered if history was repeating itself. Stock tanks and creek beds dried up. Lake levels dipped dangerously low. Livestock suffered. One rancher noted the state's climatologist's office reported, "The drought of 1956 was of longer duration, but its intensity was not as extreme."[204]

Men at First Baptist Church in Kerrville grew burdened about the situation. They recognized drought jeopardized the livestock and livelihood of ranchers in the Texas Hill Country. They recognized their neighbors needed water, and they committed the matter to prayer.

The men felt God leading them to deliver water to neighbors in need. Before long, the church received two 300-gallon tanks, and a member of the congregation donated the use of a trailer. Another layman made a pump and generator available for use. With all the donated goods and services, the ministry cost the church only $100, but its impact was felt throughout the region. Members delivered water to one woman who was caring for 13 children. They met the needs of a rancher who had been without water four days. They repaired a well for one resident. In all, the Baptist Men delivered water 50 times in a short time before much-anticipated rain finally fell. They presented the gospel every time they made a delivery, and at least one person made a profession of faith in Jesus Christ. "God called men to see how they can be used where they are to touch lives," TBM Executive Director Leo Smith said.[205]

---

204. *Browning Ranch Journal*, "The South Central Texas Drought of 2008-2009," Fall 2009, http://www.clbrowningranch.org/journal/2010/02/the-south-central-texas-drought-of-2008-2009-1.html.

205. *2009 Texas Baptist Annual*, p. 214.

Typhoon relief in the Philippines

In September 2009, the Philippines received in overabundance what ranchers in Central Texas had craved for months. Twin typhoons Ketsana and Parma hit the island, causing extensive flooding. In some areas, water rose more than 20 feet, and 80 percent of Manila was underwater at one point. Ketsana alone claimed 246 lives in the Philippines, the National Disaster Coordinating Council reported. At the invitation of Baptist Global Response, 10 TBM volunteers journeyed to the Philippines to assist with relief operations. The TBM volunteers worked alongside Kentucky Baptist Men, Oklahoma Baptist Men and volunteers with the Southern Baptist Convention of Texas. A major part of the volunteers' mission involved not only training local people in disaster response, but also helping

Volunteers in a TBM disaster relief field kitchen prepare meals that will be distributed in insulated containers called cambros.

them learn how to cope with the trauma. "Imagine standing in two or three inches of muck and having to dig it out, remove furniture, remove personal belongings, decide what to save and what to throw out, and then rinse off and sanitize what is left," said Dick Talley, logistics coordinator for TBM disaster relief. "It is quite emotional for those who are going through it."[206]

When the Baptist volunteers arrived, they learned the Filipino government reported 6 million people had been affected by the flooding, and 287,000 remained housed in shelters. They discovered waist-deep stagnant water in

---

206. BGCT Communications, "Texas Baptist Men sending relief team to the Philippines," Oct. 5, 2009, https://www.baptiststandard.com/news/texas/10174-texas-baptist-men-sending-relief-team-to-the-philippines.

some locations, providing a breeding ground for disease. Huge piles of debris remained in city streets. "The immenseness of the damage and the number of people that it has affected is overwhelming," said Larry Vawter, a TBM volunteer from Altair. "There is so much work to be done here. Yet, you still see children playing and having fun. We're able to play with them and put a smile on their face, hopefully bringing a little bit of respite among all this mess."[207]

As one of their first assignments, the Baptist volunteers removed mud and muck from the home of a bivocational pastor and his family, as well as from the church they serve across the street from the parsonage. Felicisimo Cables first learned about the danger of rising water in a text message from his daughter. He rushed home to warn his wife, Marieta, only to discover the road near his home blocked. In desperation, he swam through about 800 meters of raging water, passing submerged automobiles, debris from buildings and countless possessions from thousands of flooded homes. When he arrived at his house, he found it full of water. "I still have my family and my faith, which is what matters and what got me through," Cables told a reporter. Still, he talked about missing a Bible filled with notes a missionary had given him 17 years earlier. So, TBM volunteer Ernie Rice of Stockdale gave the pastor his own Bible.[208]

In addition to teaching by example the "mud-out" process to Filipinos, some of the Baptist volunteers accompanied missionaries to deliver food in some of the poorest areas hit by the floods. In one instance, they brought the first aid the area had received in two weeks. At that particular location, seven people made professions of faith in Christ.[209]

Killer Earthquake devastates Haiti

On Jan. 12, 2010, a 7.0 magnitude earthquake hit Haiti's capital city of Port-au-Prince, affecting more than 3 million people. Thousands lost their homes and were left without clean water and sufficient food. Within 48 hours, Texas Baptist Men provided 5,000 water purification systems for Haiti and loaded them on a C-130 military transport plane at Carswell Air Base. TBM received a $10,000 grant from the Texas Baptist Offering for World Hunger to help the organization with its rapid response.[210] Paramount Baptist Church

207. Rand Jenkins, "Texas Baptist Men offer relief and hope after Philippines flooding," *Baptist Standard*, Oct. 19, 2009, p. 2.

208. *Ibid.*

209. *Ibid.*

210. "Baptists respond to needs in Haiti after killer quake devastates capital," Jan. 14, 2010, https://www.baptiststandard.com/news/texas/10605-baptists-respond-to-needs-in-haiti-after-killer-quake-devastates-capital.

in Amarillo sent all money received in offerings from their Saturday and Sunday services one weekend—$63,000—to TBM for disaster relief in Haiti. The offering was exactly the amount needed to enable TBM to deliver the water filters, TBM Executive Director Leo Smith said. Paramount Pastor Gil Lane had been preaching a series of sermons on living passionately. "Part of

living passionately is doing something drastic," he said, and members of his congregation—about half of them trained TBM disaster relief volunteers—decided to take drastic action to help TBM make a difference in Haiti.[211]

After some delays, the plane loaded with water purifiers finally received clearance to enter Haiti Jan. 26, and a TBM disaster relief team trained in water

Ernie Rice, a Texas Baptist Men volunteer from First Baptist Church in Stockdale, joins Haitian volunteers in "antpiling"— working like an army of ants to move small pieces of rubble from a building site, one piece at a time, during a 2011 building project near Petit Goave, Haiti.

purification left the United States for Haiti the next day. The team planned to concentrate efforts on providing pure water for a medical clinic and several orphanages, Smith noted. At about the same time, Baylor Health Care System also sent a medical team to Haiti, entering the country on a corporate jet on loan from Mike Roberts, a member of Park Cities Baptist Church in Dallas.[212]

When the TBM team arrived, they discovered Haitians whose homes had been destroyed by the earthquake had set up makeshift shelters using sheets, blankets, sticks and string. Few of the tent cities had access to clean drinking water. More than 30 orphanages lacked food, water or both. Within days after the TBM hit the ground in Haiti, they installed a water purification system at the church-operated Grace Village orphanage and hospital, providing clean water for more than 100 orphans. Soon after the water filtration system was in place, James Cundiff—a TBM volunteer from McKinney—arranged for

211. John Hall, "Amarillo church gives entire weekend offering to TBM Haiti relief project," *Baptist Standard*, Feb. 1, 2010, p. 12.

212. John Hall, "Specialized Texas Baptist teams enter Haiti to offer relief," *Baptist Standard,* Feb. 1, 2010, pp. 2, 10.

the delivery of more than 27,000 meals for the orphans and for about 19,000 people living in a tent city near Grace Village.[213] A short time later, Cundiff formed We Care Haiti, a Christian nonprofit organization dedicated to helping the people of Haiti recover. [214]

Several months later, TBM helped a group of disabled Haitians achieve a dream, spurred on by Fred Sorrells from First Baptist Church in Kingsland. Sorrells, founding president of the International Institute of Sport, wanted to help disabled people in Haiti recognize their value in God's sight. "In Haiti, to be disabled is to be castoff. The general feeling is, 'Why don't you just go off somewhere and die?'" he said.[215] Sorrells discovered Haiti's national soccer team was in Texas, and he went to Frisco to meet them. He found out the team's captain, Pierre Bruny, was a devout Christian. Sorrells presented Bruny with his vision—to put together an amputee soccer team from Haiti that could compete at the World Amputee Soccer Association's World Cup in Crespo, Argentina.

When Bruny returned to Haiti, he visited hospitals to invite amputees to try out for a national amputee soccer team, and he assembled the team by mid-August. Although securing birth certificates, passports and visas was challenging in a nation where many personal records had been destroyed by an earthquake, Bruny eventually helped the team obtain all the necessary documents to travel internationally. TBM stepped in to provide airfare for the team. Several members of the team became Christians, and TBM made plans to train them in water purification. "The first casualty of disaster is hope," said Dick Talley, disaster relief logistics coordinator for TBM. "They're going to be able to tell other earthquake survivors that there is hope, that there is life after an earthquake, and they are proof of it." [216]

During the summer of 2011, 10 TBM volunteers journeyed to Haiti to clear rubble where an earthquake destroyed the facilities of Croix Hillaire Baptist Church and school near Petit Goave. The TBM crew worked alongside members of the church to prepare a site where additional teams could help the Haitians rebuild. When a small front-end loader the crew had rented refused to work, the volunteers worked "like an army of ants, moving little pieces one at a time," said Ernie Rice, mission team leader and member of First Baptist Church in Stockdale. "Our goal from the beginning was

213. John Hall, "Relief slow in Haiti, but hope is emerging," *Baptist Standard*, Feb. 15, 2010, p. 2.

214. http://www.wecarehaitiministries.org/who-we-are/.

215. George Henson, "TBM helps Haitian amputee soccer team achieve a dream," *Baptist Standard*, Oct. 25, 2010, p. 3.

216. *Ibid.*

to build relationships with the church there and encourage the church as it reaches out to its community. The challenge was making those relationships click. When we started working together, it all started to gel. That Bobcat we rented never functioned, but that made us all pitch in and work together. It got the whole church involved in antpiling."[217] In the process, something unexpected happened. Rice fell in love with Haiti and its people. He began to make frequent trips to Haiti, working closely with ongoing Baptist General Convention of Texas recovery efforts. In 2014, he and his wife, Sharon, moved there to work with We Care Haiti.[218] Later, they became missionaries to Haiti, appointed by their home church, South Central Baptist Area and the BGCT.

Before Rice became involved with ministries in Haiti, he journeyed with TBM to Chile to lead a disaster relief team who ministered there after an earthquake rocked the nation. Rice and his crew found 10 Chilean pastors living in tents near where their homes once stood. Although it was spring 2010 in Texas, winter was approaching in the Southern Hemisphere, and it was raining. "They're in a high degree of misery," Rice reported.[219] So, TBM took up the challenge to build houses for the pastors.

217. Ken Camp, "TBM volunteers see God's wisdom and God's intervention in Haiti," Aug. 7, 2011, https://www.baptiststandard.com/news/texas/12847-tbm-volunteers-see-gods-wisdom-a-gods-intervention-in-haiti.

218. Ken Camp, "Care for Haiti leads Stockdale couple to full-time missions," May 7, 2014, https://www.baptiststandard.com/news/texas/16434-care-for-haiti-leads-stockdale-couple-to-full-time-missions.

219. John Hall, "Chilean pastors living in tents as winter approaches," *Baptist Standard*, May 24, 2010, p. 20.

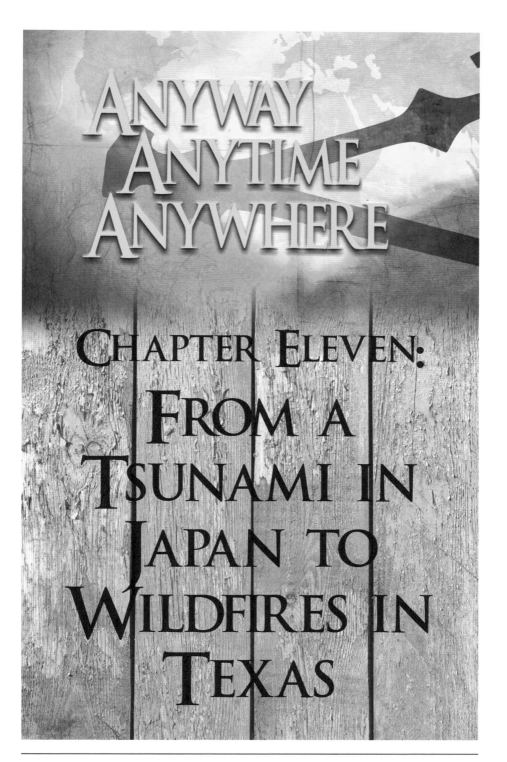

ANYWAY ANYTIME ANYWHERE

CHAPTER ELEVEN:

FROM A TSUNAMI IN JAPAN TO WILDFIRES IN TEXAS

CHAPTER ELEVEN:
FROM A TSUNAMI IN JAPAN TO WILDFIRES IN TEXAS

Earthquake and tsunami devastate Japan

On March 11, 2011, Japan experienced a magnitude 9.1 earthquake that spawned a killer tsunami. The earthquake was so intense, it moved the Japanese island of Honshu eight feet eastward, and 250 miles of its coastline dropped two feet. Confirmed deaths topped 15,800, and the disaster left 2,500 missing. The Japanese government estimated $300 billion in property damage. The tsunami also caused a cooling system failure at the Fukushima Daiichi nuclear power plant, leading to a Level-7 meltdown and the release of radioactive materials.[220]

The Baptist General Convention of Texas committed $25,000 to relief and recovery efforts in Japan, working with the Japanese Baptist Convention, Baptist World Aid, the Southern Baptist Convention's International Mission Board and the Cooperative Baptist Fellowship, and Texas Baptist Men prepared to send an advance team to work with the Japanese Baptists.[221]

When the first Texas Baptist team—veteran TBM disaster relief leaders Gary Smith and John LaNoue, together with Yukata Takarada, pastor of the Japanese Baptist Church of Dallas, and Rex Campbell, videographer with the Baptist General Convention of Texas—arrived in Japan, they delivered kerosene, rice and noodles to three churches in a hard-hit Sendai area. The team had learned from Japan Baptist Convention representatives about difficulties in obtaining fuel—both gasoline and kerosene. "After consulting with the leaders, it was determined that taking kerosene and some easily prepared food to the people in the Sendai area would meet an immediate need," Takarada said. "It was received with great joy."[222]

In addition to delivering the fuel and food, the Texas crew also brought Geiger counters, to enable the people to determine their level of radiation exposure—and so the Texans could find out their own level of risk. At the end of the week in Japan, the crew found out their level of exposure to

---

220. https://www.livescience.com/39110-japan-2011-earthquake-tsunami-facts.html.

221. "Texas Baptists commit $25,000 to Japanese relief effort," March 13, 2011, https://www.baptiststandard.com/news/texas/12306-texas-baptists-commit-25000-to-japanese-relief-effort.

222. "Texas Baptists deliver kerosene, food to Japanese churches," April 6, 2011, https://www.baptiststandard.com/news/texas/12373-texas-baptists-delivers-kerosene-food-to-japanese-churches.

---

radiation was roughly equal to going through a CT scan or MRI. "A fire chief, who was Baptist, took us where it was the worst," LaNoue recalled later.[223] The Texans witnessed "total destruction," Smith said. "We saw a school where young children had been released early, and all were swept away. Older children were taken to the roof, where they were rescued," he recalled. "We helped the people get a handle on the chaos, as best we could."[224]

One woman told the Texas crew the story of her parents' death, based on the testimony of people who witnessed it from a hilltop. The people on the hill called out to the woman's parents, seeking to warn them, but the couple could not outrun the tsunami. One of their bodies was found, and the other was listed as missing and presumed dead. The Texas team also met a pastor who was inside his house when the earthquake hit. Although the rest of the family fled outside the house, the pastor's son was paralyzed with fear, crouched under a table. The pastor ran inside the house, even while it was shaking. Shielding his son with his own body, he led the boy to safety. "This father's love reminds me of the love of God demonstrated toward us," Takarada wrote later. "He himself gave up his life in order to deliver us. ... Even today, Jesus is with us, holding our hands and saying, 'Son, I am with you always.' My prayer is that people who are in trouble out of this tragic event come to know that Jesus is searching for them and calling out, saying, 'Where are you?' If anyone says: 'I am here, Jesus. I am scared,' then I am very sure that Jesus will approach those who are crying out to him and stretch his hand out and hold his hand and say, 'Do not be troubled, my son, because I am here with you, and I will never leave you nor forsake you.'"[225]

While the crew served in Japan, stateside TBM volunteers loaded 2,000 water filters on a crate bound for Japan, along with medical supplies donated by Baylor Health Care System and its Faith in Action Initiative. Baylor provided the supplies for the University of Tokyo Institute of Medicine, as well as for the Japan Baptist Convention to distribute as needed. The water filters were capable not only of filtering out dirt and other solid pollutants, but also removing all but 0.2 microns of radiation from water, making it safe to drink. While LaNoue and Smith were in Japan, they trained convention leaders how to use the filters, so they would be prepared to teach pastors and others once the shipment arrived.[226]

---

223. Interview with John LaNoue in Frost, Texas, Oct. 20, 2015.

224. Interview with Gary Smith in Dallas, Texas, Oct. 2, 2015.

225. "Texas Baptists deliver kerosene, food to Japanese churches," April 6, 2011.

226. *Ibid.*

About a month after the crew returned to Texas, TBM and the BGCT provided funds for a van for the Japan Baptist Convention to use, transporting people and supplies into areas affected by the disaster. "Unlike most churches and individuals in the United States, many Japanese do not own personal or church vehicles," said Chris Liebrum, leader of the BGCT disaster response program. "Most people use the advanced mass transit systems. However, current conditions require that the Japan Baptist Convention have the ability to not only be more flexible with their transportation, but to have vehicles that they can use to haul supplies, such as food and cooking equipment to the areas around Sendai. Japanese leaders also need these types of vehicles to transport relief workers both from their country and others who will come to Japan to help with the relief."[227]

Ministry in the aftermath of wildfires

While a TBM advance team served in tsunami-soaked Japan, other TBM volunteers responded to devastation caused by more than 90 wildfires that swept across much of Texas, charring about a million acres. One of those wildfires destroyed the sanctuary of First Baptist Church of Possum Kingdom Lake, along with the church nursery, office and kitchen. Pastor Dennis Trammel learned about the fire when he was returning from vacation. At about 3 p.m. on April 15, a church member called to say the church's parsonage appeared to be in danger of burning. Four hours later, another caller reassured him the parsonage had escaped harm. But then about 8:30 p.m., when he was just a few miles from the church, he received another call, and he learned the church was engulfed in flames. "They had personnel there. They had equipment there. They were putting water on it, but it still caught," Trammell said.[228] Two days later, the congregation met for worship in the church's family life center, which firefighters had saved from the blaze. In the middle of the worship service, the fire marshal evacuated the city due to approaching wildfires.

TBM disaster relief emergency food-service crews prepared meals for affected residents and firefighters at Possum Kingdom Lake, Aspermont and Fort Davis. They also sent ash-out crews to help clean up in Fort Davis. "We're trying to show the presence of God to the victims of the fires," Dick Talley, TBM disaster relief logistics coordinator, told a Texas Baptist reporter.

---

227. "Texas Baptists to provide van for Japan tsunami relief effort," May 18, 2011, https://www.baptiststandard.com/news/texas/12543-texas-baptists-to-provide-van-for-japan-tsunami-relief-effort .

228. "Wildfires destroy church facility; TBM serves affected region," April 18, 2011, https://www.baptiststandard.com/news/texas/12432-wildfires-destroy-church-facility-tbm-serves-affected-region.

"That can be through feeding or helping them clean out their property, find personal belongings—whatever it takes to help those individuals affected by the fires."[229] "Whatever it takes" included collecting bottled water for firefighters who were battling wildfires and for residents who were working on their fire-damaged property. In three days, TBM collected 3,511 cases of bottled water and began distributing it. One woman was so determined to contribute to the cause that she carried two cases of bottled water with her on a cross-town bus ride and then walked another two miles to deliver it to the Dixon Missions Equipping Center in east Dallas, TBM Associate Executive Director Mickey Lenamon reported.[230] By early May, TBM collected more than 4,000 cases of water. Meanwhile, emergency food-service crews served meals in Junction City and Comstock and recovery volunteers from Dallas County Cowboy Church worked in Fort Davis, delivering snacks and supplies to firefighters in Strawn on their way.[231]

Wildfires continued to cause property damage and endanger lives throughout 2011, as the state experienced the worst one-year drought since Texas began keeping records of such matters in 1895. The Texas A&M Forest Service reported 2,947 homes destroyed by 31,453 wildfires that consumed 4 million acres in a season deemed "unique in scope, duration and complexity."[232] Wildfires destroyed homes in more than half of Texas' 254 counties, but the worst damage occurred in Bastrop County. The Bastrop Complex fire Sept. 4 destroyed 1,660 homes, consumed 32,400 acres and burned for 37 days.[233]

Leticia Lybarger was among the affected homeowners. When the fire approached her home, she and other family members quickly grabbed as many of their belongings as possible and stuffed them into their vehicles before they escaped the blaze. The day she returned to her uninsured home, the sight of the utter devastation overwhelmed her. "I fell to the ground," she said. "But the minute I hit that ground, I had three people holding on to me and praying, saying, 'It's OK.'" The trio who offered her comfort were members of her church, Primera Iglesia Bautista in Bastrop. The church also provided food and temporary lodging for her family, along with gift cards

229. *Ibid.*

230. John Hall, "TBM collects more than 3,500 cases of water for wildfire relief," April 26, 2011, https://www.baptiststandard.com/news/texas/12467-tbm-collects-more-than-3500-cases-of-water-for-wildfire-relief.

231. Ken Camp, "TBM continues to meet needs in Texas," May 5, 2011, https://www.baptiststandard.com/news/texas/12483-tbm-continues-to-meet-needs-in-texas.

232. Justice Jones, April Saginor and Brad Smith, "2011 Texas Wildfires: Common Denominators of Home Destruction," Texas A&M Forest Service, http://texasforestservice.tamu.edu/uploadedFiles/FRP/New_-_Mitigation/Safety_Tips/2011%20Texas%20Wildfires.pdf.

233. *Ibid.*

to purchase what they needed as they began to put their lives back together. The congregation cooked meals in the church kitchen for more than 50 people a day and housed up to 10 displaced families in Sunday school rooms. Richard Shahan, pastor of Calvary Baptist Church in Bastrop, also lost his home to the fire, along with at least seven other families in his congregation. Even so, he worked as a police chaplain, offering comfort and counsel to overwhelmed officers in the days after the fire started. Meanwhile, TBM disaster relief volunteers were deployed to Bastrop, and food-service crews worked 24-hour shifts to prepare about 5,000 meals a day for firefighters.[234] "Most are volunteer firefighters," Dick Talley told a reporter for the *San Angelo Standard Times*. "They are all tired and worn out."[235]

At Timberline Fellowship, TBM volunteers provided meals, as well as access to showers and laundry units. The congregation served as a base for ministry in spite of its losses. The fire burned the pastor's library, melted siding on the exterior of its sanctuary and its education building and destroyed lawn equipment and office supplies stored in two small mobile buildings that burned. The parsonage and the church building also sustained smoke damage. Of the 34 families in the congregation, 16 lost their homes and all their possessions, but everyone survived. "All church members came out safe," Pastor Gordon Friday said. "That's all I care about. Everything else can be replaced sooner or later."[236]

Within a few months, TBM worked with Timberline Fellowship to bring rebirth and restoration to the area. TBM borrowed a portable sawmill from East Texas Baptist Encampment. Volunteers turned usable portions of wildfire-charred timber into lumber for building projects, cutting and sorting it. Then they provided the lumber, along with building plans for a storage building, to homeowners. They also made the lumber available to homeowners for porches and ramps. One couple brought a tree to the TBM sawmill, saying the woman's grandfather planted it 47 years earlier. They used a portion of the lumber from the tree for their own reconstruction project and donated the rest to help others in the community. "It broke our hearts to see all the timber lost in disaster. I'm glad we have found a way to

234. John Hall, "As wildfires rage, Texas Baptists minister to hurting neighbors," Sept. 6, 2011, https://www.baptiststandard.com/news/texas/12953-as-wildfires-rage-texas-baptists-minister-to-hurting-neighbors.

235. Matthew Waller, "Texas Baptists minister to needs caused by Texas wildfires," Sept. 11, 2011, https://www.baptiststandard.com/news/texas/12987-texas-baptists-minister-to-needs-caused-by-texas-wildfires.

236. John Hall, "Despite damage, Bastrop-area church serves community," Sept. 22, 2011, https://www.baptiststandard.com/news/texas/13016-despite-damage-bastrop-area-church-serves-community.

capture some of it for kingdom use," said Jim Long, a TBM volunteer from Snow Hill Baptist Church in Mount Pleasant.[237]

TBM volunteers put to good use the experience they gained in the wake of the 2011 wildfires when neighboring states experienced similar disasters the following year. In mid-July 2012, TBM teams worked in New Mexico, removing ash and debris from burned out homes and helping homeowners reclaim any possessions salvaged from the fires. One woman asked the TBM crew to help her look for several items with sentimental value to her family—wedding rings that belonged to her and her husband, antique guns, jewelry and ceramic angels. The crew worked several hours, but they eventually located all of the treasured possessions. Intense heat had melted several items, but the wedding rings emerged in good condition. "The lady cried, and the team cried with her," said Joe Henard, a TBM volunteer from Paramount Baptist Church in Amarillo. His team presented each family with whom they worked a new treasured possession—a leather-bound Bible, donated by Sunday school classes at the Amarillo church. Several weeks later, TBM volunteers responded to similar needs in northeastern Oklahoma, where wildfires affected more than 300 homes.[239]

Hurricanes in Louisiana and the Northeast

While the Southwest suffered drought and resultant wildfires, other parts of the country felt the effects of hurricanes in 2012. A tropical depression began to form east of the Lesser Antilles on Aug. 21. It soon grew to become Tropical Storm Isaac as it made its way westward through the Caribbean and into the Gulf of Mexico before reaching hurricane status off the coast of southeast Louisiana. When it made landfall Aug. 28, it packed sustained 80 mph winds and dumped rain on the southern part of the state.[240]

While the hurricane was still in the Gulf of Mexico, TBM placed disaster relief volunteers on standby in anticipation of a major deployment.[241] An

---

237. "Sawmill ministry brings hope out of charred timber," Jan. 31, 2012, https://www. baptiststandard.com/news/texas/13446-sawmill-ministry-brings-hope-out-of-charred-timber.

238. George Henson, "Texas Baptist Men volunteers head to New Mexico to help with ash-out efforts," July 19, 2012, https://www.baptiststandard.com/news/texas/14050-texas-baptist-men-volunteers-head-to-new-mexico-to-help-with-ash-out-efforts.

239. John Hall, "Texas Baptist Men volunteers respond to Oklahoma wildfires," Aug. 15, 2012, https://www.baptiststandard.com/news/texas/14163-texas-baptist-men-volunteers-respond-to-oklahoma-wildfires.

240. National Weather Service, "Hurricane Isaac—August 29, 2012," https://www.weather.gov/mob/isaac.

241. Ken Camp, "Update: About 100 TBM volunteers ready to help after Hurricane Isaac," Aug. 27, 2012, https://www.baptiststandard.com/news/texas/14216-update-about-100-tbm-volunteers-ready-to-help-after-hurricane-isaac.

advance team left Dallas Aug. 31 to help coordinate the multistate Southern Baptist disaster relief response. Terry Henderson, TBM state disaster relief director, coordinated responders from Texas, Louisiana, Arkansas, Oklahoma and Missouri from the Southern Baptist disaster relief command center at First Baptist Church in Covington, La. He worked with Joe Henard from Paramount Baptist Church in Amarillo, who was the command center's logistics and safety officer; Ralph Rogers, also from Paramount in Amarillo, who was operations officer; and Cindy Wesch form Hillcrest Baptist Church

in Midlothian, who served as administrative officer. Ray Gann, a TBM volunteer from Whitesboro, worked as a liaison between the American Red Cross, Southern Baptist disaster relief field kitchens and grocery providers.[242]

Terry Henderson (right) joined the TBM staff in 2012 as state disaster relief director. He consults with Gary Smith, longtime disaster relief volunteer, in the command center in Dallas.

Henderson had joined the TBM staff about five months earlier. He had served as national relief director for the Southern Baptist Convention's North American Mission Board from June 2003 to December 2010. Previously, he worked 28 years with the Orange County Fire/Rescue Division in Florida, and was volunteer cleanup and recovery coordinator for the Florida Baptist Convention's disaster relief ministry for 10 years.[243]

Throughout September 2012, TBM deployed volunteers to serve in Louisiana. Food-service crews worked from the field kitchen of the state Disaster Relief Mobile Unit set up at Belle Chasse Baptist Church in Algiers, La., to prepare meals for storm survivors and emergency personnel. Mud-out crews from University Baptist Church in Houston, Colorado Baptist

242. Ken Camp, "TBM team to coordinate multi-state disaster response in Louisiana," Aug. 30, 2012, https://www.baptiststandard.com/news/texas/14226-tbm-team-to-coordinate-multi-state-disaster-response-in-louisiana.

243. "Henderson named TBM disaster relief director," March 20, 2012, https://www.baptiststandard.com/news/texas/13621-henderson-named-tbm-disaster-relief-director.

Association and Collin Baptist Association helped residents in the region remove muck, damaged drywall and soaked flooring from homes. Shower and laundry units from Comanche, Tyler, O'Donnell, Austin Baptist Association, Gambrell Baptist Association and Denton Baptist Association provided service to National Guard personnel, American Red Cross volunteers and a variety of other first-responders in the area. At Celebration Church in LaPlace, La., a TBM crew from Smith Baptist Association set up food-service operations, while Victim Relief Ministries set up a trailer and displayed a banner designating its unit as a "prayer station" for anyone who wanted to pray.[244] By mid-September, the food-service crew in Algiers had prepared about 10,000 meals, and two additional shower and laundry units were called into service.[245]

Several weeks after TBM completed disaster relief in Louisiana, volunteers were called into service again. Tropical Storm Sandy formed in the Central Caribbean in mid-October and grew to hurricane strength as it made its way across Jamaica, Cuba and the Bahamas and then began its trek northward. "The track of Sandy resulted in a worse case scenario for storm surge for coastal regions from New Jersey north to Connecticut, including New York City and Long Island," the National Weather Service reported. "Unfortunately, the storm surge occurred near the time of high tide along the Atlantic Coast. This contributed to record tide levels."[246] Media on the East Coast labeled the hurricane "Superstorm Sandy." About 100 TBM volunteers participated in a multi-state Southern Baptist disaster relief mission to the densely populated region. Altogether, about 900 Southern Baptist volunteers from 27 states and Canada responded. Terry Henderson worked as Southern Baptist disaster relief liaison at the New York City office of emergency management. TBM set up a field kitchen at Floyd Bennett Field in southeast Brooklyn at the request of the Federal Emergency Management Agency. They prepared about 10,000 meals for police officers, military personnel, other first-responders and sanitation workers. After TBM's state mobile unit and its field kitchen ended operations and started making the journey back to Texas Nov. 14, more than 20 TBM volunteers stayed behind to work

244. Ken Camp, "TBM disaster response deploys 16 units to Louisiana," Sept. 4, 2012, https://www.baptiststandard.com/news/texas/14264-tbm-disaster-response-deploys-16-units-in-louisiana.

245. Ken Camp, "TBM disaster relief sends 18 units to Louisiana," Sept. 12, 2012, https://www.baptiststandard.com/news/texas/14281-tbm-disaster-relief-sends-18-units-in-louisiana.

246. National Weather Service, "Hurricane Sandy—Oct. 29, 2012," https://www.weather.gov/okx/HurricaneSandy.

with Kentucky Baptists, who prepared meals at the Aqueduct Racetrack in Queens.[247]

A TBM mud-out crew worked in Port Monmouth, New Jersey, where the hurricane had ripped away part of the exterior wall of Port Monmouth Community Church, exposing the sanctuary to a 13-foot storm surge. The congregation lost its organ, its sound system, a piano, a refrigerator, a water heater, two pulpits and many hymnals, Bibles and other books. Church members gathered on a Saturday morning to assess damage and start cleaning up, as best they could. "We were walking around in shock trying to figure out where to start when the Texas Baptist Men pulled up in their pickup trucks with their long trailer filled with tools and supplies and introduced themselves, telling us they were the mud-out group here to clean out our church for us," Wanda Wohlin, ministry assistant to Pastor Don Magaw, wrote on her Facebook page. Magaw subsequently reprinted her post as part of his column in a church newsletter. The TBM crew worked three days, removing damaged sheetrock and power-washing and disinfecting floors and other surfaces. They also reclaimed the church's utility shed that had floated down the street, fully loaded, and placed it back where it belonged. The volunteers also replaced an electrical meter and electrical wiring that had been damaged by the storm. "I don't know how they heard of us," Wohlin wrote. "But they are angels sent from God."[248]

247. Ken Camp, "TBM joins in multistate Hurricane Sandy disaster relief," Nov. 15, 2012, https://www.baptiststandard.com/news/texas/14519-tbm-joins-in-multistate-hurricane-sandy-disaster-relief.

248. Ken Camp, "Angels from Texas minister to New Jersey church," Nov. 26, 2012, https://www.baptiststandard.com/news/texas/14631-angels-from-texas-minister-to-new-jersey-church.

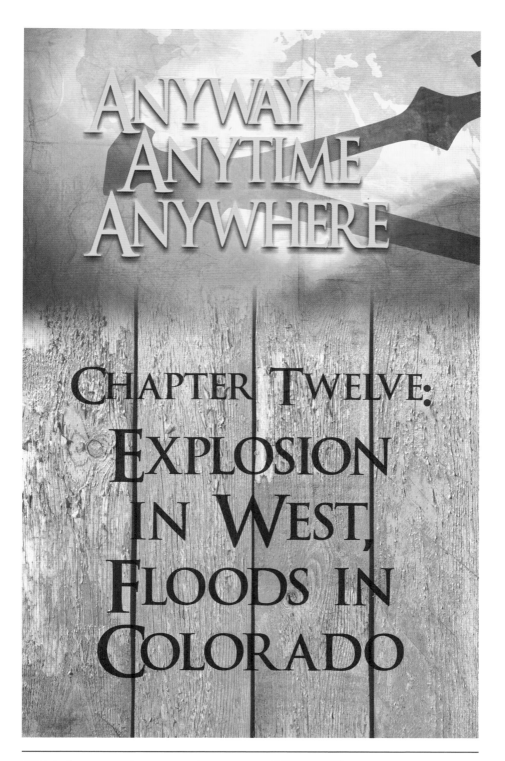

CHAPTER TWELVE:

EXPLOSION IN WEST, FLOODS IN COLORADO

Chapter Twelve: Explosion in West, Floods in Colorado

The blast that rocked a Central Texas town

Prior to April 17, 2013, many people who knew the Central Texas town of West at all thought of it primarily as a place to stop during Interstate 35 road trips for a snack of Czech bakery treats—kolaches, klobasnek and strudels.

Before deployment, TBM disaster relief volunteers gather in a circle for prayer.

That all changed at 7:50 p.m. when a fire at the West Fertilizer Company triggered an ammonium nitrate explosion. The blast claimed 15 lives—including a dozen first responders—and injured about 300 people. It destroyed 500 homes and left a 93-foot-wide and 12-foot-deep crater.[249] The explosion damaged the worship center at First Baptist Church in West, and it destroyed the home of Pastor John Crowder and his family. Crowder and his wife, Lisa, were driving home from a regional track meet in Bryan involving their daughter, Ashley, when his cell phone began ringing. They began to hear reports about the impact. "We had Royal Ambassadors who were playing kickball outside the church who were knocked to the ground. That tells you something about the force of the explosion," Crowder said.[250] Associate Pastor Phil Immicke

---

249. Bureau of Alcohol, Tobacco, Firearms and Explosives, "ATF Announces $50,000 Reward in West, Texas Fatality Fire," May 11, 2016, https://www.atf.gov/news/pr/atf-announces-50000-reward-west-texas-fatality-fire.

250. Ken Camp, "Disaster relief and recovery combine to help West heal," June 16, 2014, https://www.baptiststandard.com/news/texas/16585-disaster-relief-and-recovery-combine-to-heal-stricken-community.

helped connect parents and children, and he made the church's van available to authorities who needed to evacuate nursing home residents from a facility near the blast site.

On the first Sunday after the blast, Crowder led an open-air worship service a few days later, preaching from Psalm 46 and assuring worshippers God is the refuge for those who suffer loss. "When you reach the point where you are on your knees crying for help, you have just reached the

Volunteers with the Ellis Baptist Association box unit distribute boxes for disaster survivors to use to collect and store scattered possessions.

point of your greatest strength," Crowder told the crowd.[251] Texas Baptist Men disaster relief volunteers were present at the worship service. They had arrived in West early the morning after the blast, and they immediately contacted Crowder to find out where they could serve best. "They had boots on the ground, providing relief with their volunteers," Crowder said.[252] TBM set up a mobile laundry and shower unit, volunteers operated emergency childcare, and they distributed cardboard boxes to residents once they were allowed back into the affected area to sift through debris and reclaim keepsakes. In the first 12 days after the blast, TBM crews prepared more than 13,000 meals from an emergency food-service unit set up on the First Baptist Church property.[253] Some TBM heavy-equipment operators also gained their first experience demolishing homes in West, providing a service that

251. John Hall, "First Baptist Church in West urges members to lean on God," April 22, 2013, https://www.baptiststandard.com/news/texas/14989-first-baptist-church-in-west-urges-members-to-lean-on-god.

252. Camp, "Disaster relief and recovery combine," June 16, 2014.

253. "Texas Tidbits: TBM helps West residents," May 6, 2013, https://www.baptiststandard.com/news/texas/15035-texas-tidbits-tbm-help-residents-of-west.

saved homeowners thousands of dollars.[254] During their time in West, TBM volunteers prepared 15,791 meals, distributed 12,108 cardboard boxes, cared for 142 children, provided access to 418 showers and washed 989 loads of laundry.[255]

TBM volunteers help community members in West with their laundry.

After TBM wrapped up immediate disaster relief, the Baptist General Convention of Texas assumed responsibility for long-term disaster recovery. "There is a big difference in relief and recovery," TBM Executive Director Don Gibson said. "If you are in a serious accident, you go immediately to a doctor to get some immediate relief, help and comfort. Weeks or months later, you start your long-term recovery. Both treatments are necessary—but different."[256] BGCT representatives worked in concert with the local long-term recovery committee, on which Crowder served. Texas Baptists provided a volunteer coordinator who worked in West several months to manage the logistics of linking short-term volunteers to specific projects. The BGCT sponsored "Loving West," a one-week volunteer event in the summer that drew participants from about 650 churches around Texas who cleared debris and prepared home sites for reconstruction. Experienced construction workers involved in Texas Baptists' Shalom Builders program also worked alongside college students during spring break.

Nancy Smith, a member of First Baptist Church in San Marcos, was among the Texas Baptists who responded to the call to help West as part of the

254. Camp, "Disaster relief and recovery combine," June 16, 2014.

255. Ken Camp, "From Granbury to Oklahoma, TBM responds to disasters," May 24, 2013, https://www.baptiststandard.com/news/texas/15111-from-granbury-to-oklahoma-tbm-responds-to-disasters.

256. *Ibid.*

"Loving West" emphasis. Two years later, she and her husband, Larkin, found themselves on the receiving end of assistance after a disaster. They were visiting family in Baytown on May 24, 2015, when they learned the Blanco River had overflowed. When they returned to San Marcos, they discovered their home—about three-quarters of a mile from the river—had

FIRST BAPTIST CHURCH

GOD IS BIGGER THAN THIS!

First Baptist Church in West offers an encouraging message to a hurting town.

been flooded, along with more than a dozen other houses on their cul-de-sac. Five feet of water had filled their home, and their homeowner's insurance policy did not cover flood damage. As soon as the floodwaters receded, members of First Baptist Church in San Marcos immediately when to work on the Smith's home, ripping out soaked carpet and removing mud-stained drywall. When a TBM mud-out crew arrived, they found many of the early steps in the cleanup process already had been completed. So, the TBM crew went to work power-washing and disinfecting surfaces and clearing debris. Bill Means, a member of First Baptist Church in West, served as a TBM volunteer chaplain in San Marcos after the floods. He knew volunteers from First Baptist Church in San Marcos had helped in his community. He soon found out Nancy Smith had led that team, and he learned about the damage to her home. When he called home to let people in his church know about it, the women of First Baptist in West began assembling a package of gift items—including kolaches and cookies from a Czech bakery—and sent it to San Marcos. Means delivered the package to the Smiths, who were overwhelmed at the loving gesture.[257]

As First Baptist Church in West became known increasingly as a congregation that loved its neighbors and people in need started looking for peace in the midst of upheaval, God brought revival. Crowder baptized more

257. Ken Camp, "Volunteer love connection links West and San Marcos," June 2, 2015, https://www.baptiststandard.com/news/texas/17857-volunteer-love-connection-links-west-and-san-marcos.

people in 2014 than in the previous three years combined, and attendance in weekly worship services increased significantly. "Something like this

TBM Chaplain Rachel Schieck counsels a West resident.

Members of a box unit distribute cardboard boxes to residents in West.

has a way of making people re-evaluate their priorities," he said.[258]

It also created in the church an insatiable desire to show other communities in need the kind of love they had been shown. In August 2016, when TBM volunteers were serving in flooded south Louisiana, the crews in Jennings, La., needed bottled water and sports drinks. In response, First Baptist Church spearheaded a collection drive. In less than 48 hours, West residents donated 180 cases of water and sports drinks, filling the beds of two pickup trucks. Crowder and Reggie Whalen, a layman at First Baptist in West, delivered the drinks to the Dixon Missions Equipping Center in Dallas. "As

soon as our people heard the name 'Texas Baptist Men,' they were eager to respond," Crowder said. "It brings back so many memories of what they did for us, and we're all so grateful." [259]

---

258. *Ibid.*

259. Ken Camp, "West church repays kindness, helps TBM meet needs in Louisiana," Aug. 26, 2016, https://www.baptiststandard.com/news/texas/19441-west-church-repays-kindness-helps-tbm-meet-needs-in-louisiana.

Tornadoes in Texas and Oklahoma, flooding along the Rio Grande

Less than one month after the West fertilizer plant explosion, TBM disaster relief volunteers were mobilized to respond to needs after tornadoes ripped through North Central Texas, just south of the Dallas-Fort Worth area. A series of tornadoes that touched down around Granbury and Cleburne May 15 claimed a half-dozen lives, injured dozens and left hundreds of people homeless. Two TBM-trained disaster relief volunteers—Tracey Bartley and Dan Armes—helped transport some of the injured individuals to a triage center that was set up at Acton Baptist Church in Granbury, where TBM also established its on-site disaster relief headquarters.[260] A TBM food-service crew that was still working in West sent 200 meals to first-responders in Granbury the evening the tornadoes hit. The next morning chainsaw crews began to clear tornado-tossed trees and broken limbs. A blue-tarp team from the Austin area provided temporary coverings for homes that sustained serious roof damage. [261]

In the days immediately following the tornadoes, more than 100 members of Acton Baptist church participated in on-site disaster relief training that not only equipped them to assist in debris removal and emergency food service, but also worked in crews with specially trained chainsaw operators. Within eight days of the time the tornadoes touched down, six TBM chainsaw crews completed 59 projects. Many of the chainsaw team members gave Bibles to the families they served and prayed with them, and volunteer chaplains provided spiritual counsel to more than 250 people. A shower and laundry unit setup at Acton Baptist provided access to 139 showers, and residents and volunteers washed 40 loads of laundry. TBM volunteers also provided care for 30 children and distributed boxes throughout the community to help residents collect and store their scattering belongings.

Less than a week after the tornadoes hit Granbury and the surrounding area, tornadoes swept through Oklahoma, seriously damaging Moore and Shawnee. TBM set up a command post in Shawnee and provided support to Oklahoma Baptists who concentrated their disaster relief efforts on hard-hit Moore. Five TBM heavy-equipment operators worked in Moore, helping Oklahoma Baptists remove heavy debris and load it into dumpsters. TBM chainsaw crews worked in and around Shawnee, where the tornado cut a

---

260. Camp, "From Granbury to Oklahoma, TBM responds to disasters," May 24, 2013.

261. Ken Camp, "Texas Baptist Men volunteers respond after tornadoes," May 16, 2013, https://www.baptiststandard.com/news/texas/15066-texas-baptist-men-volunteers-respond-after-tornadoes-texas-baptist-men-volunteers-respond-after-tornadoes.

60-mile swath.[262] During their time in Oklahoma, TBM volunteers worked alongside Southern Baptist disaster relief volunteers from Arkansas, Iowa, Kansas, Nebraska, Louisiana, Missouri and North Carolina, as well as Oklahoma Baptists.

In late June, more than 16 inches of rain fell in 36 hours along the Rio Grande, causing extensive flooding. TBM mud-out crews from Sabine Neches Baptist Area and Second Baptist Church in La Grange immediately went to work in Eagle Pass. The La Grange Church also made available its shower and laundry mobile unit. A crew from Denton Baptist Association distributed boxes to residents in the area, and a volunteer construction team completed 15 roofing jobs. The durable medical equipment ministry of Northeast Baptist Church in San Antonio also provided canes, walkers and wheelchairs to residents with mobility issues. TBM chaplains distributed Spanish-language New Testaments, prayed with displaced people and reported 69 professions of faith in Christ.[263]

Flooding in Colorado

In September 2013, floods disrupted lives in the West, and Texas Baptist Men responded with disaster relief. One group of TBM volunteers concentrated attention in the El Paso area, using shovels, high-pressure hoses and disinfectant to clean out 87

Texas Baptist Men disaster relief workers worked to clear debris in Jamestown, Colo., after the James River flooded the mining town northwest of Boulder.

mud-caked homes in Socorro, an El Paso suburb across the Rio Grande from Ciudad Juarez. Another 28-member group of TBM volunteers journeyed to Colorado. On their first day in Loveland, Colo., an assessment team

263. Ken Camp, "From floods to fires, disaster victims spell relief 'T-B-M,'" July 8, 2013, https://www.baptiststandard.com/news/texas/15267-from-floods-to-fires-disaster-victims-spell-relief-t-b-m.

evaluated 26 homes, but road closures limited their access to some of the worst-hit areas. Even so, mud-out teams cleaned two homes that day.[264]

When TBM Disaster Relief Director Terry Henderson and his wife, Barbara, heard about an isolated mining town northwest of Boulder in need of assistance, they made a treacherous 40-mile journey through rain, snow and over washed-out roads from Loveland to Jamestown, Colo., to assess the situation. They discovered homes devastated by the disaster and a community without water or electricity. Mounds of rock and debris filled yards, streets and—in many cases—homes. One house they visited was filled with 4 feet of sand, and the mount of debris in the resident's front yard was more than 10 feet high. Recognizing the magnitude of the need in Jamestown, TBM decided to concentrate efforts there, while North Carolina Baptist Men assumed responsibility for mud-out projects in Loveland.[265]

Mud-out crews went to work in Jamestown, but they discovered a distinctly different situation than what they typically encountered in Texas. "It's not mud as much as it's houses filled with sand, rock and gravel several feet high" that volunteers had to remove with buckets and shovels, said Judge Camp, a volunteer from First Baptist Church in Lewisville, on-site coordinator for the TBM teams. Some homes were swept off their foundations by raging water. One newlywed couple saw their home washed away and deposited as a pile of debris 100 yards from their property. TBM volunteers removed heavy debris so the couple could reclaim a few treasured belongings, including some wedding presents. Meanwhile, other volunteers focused on measures to prevent the situation from growing worse. Volunteers filled sandbags to hold back water that continued to erode the ground near some buildings, and chainsaw crews felled trees in danger of falling due to heavy erosion, as well as moving fallen limbs. Skid-steer operators followed them, using heavy machinery to remove the trees, as well as some boulders and other debris from residential areas.[266]

In addition to clearing debris from homes and roadways, TBM volunteers also removed some obstacles that separated residents from God. "People there will tell you. They moved up there to get away from church, to get

264. Ken Camp, "TBM provides disaster relief in the West," Sept. 27, 2013, https://www.baptiststandard.com/news/texas/15588-tbm-provides-disaster-relief-after-floods-in-the-west.

265. Ken Camp, "TBM disaster relief volunteers relocate to mining town," Oct. 3, 2013, https://www.baptiststandard.com/news/texas/15625-tbm-disaster-relief-volunteers-relocate-to-mining-town.

266. Ken Camp, "TBM relief workers move mud, debris in Colorado," Oct. 11, 2013, https://www.baptiststandard.com/news/texas/15653-tbm-relief-workers-move-mud-debris-in-colorado.

away from civilization and to get away from the world," Terry Henderson said, noting the TBM workers "opened up some doors to the gospel" by sticking with the people and meeting their needs. Multiple short-term volunteer groups arrived each weekend to assist the community, but the TBM crews were "embedded with the community," he noted. Since some of the Jamestown residents were miners and engineers with experience operating earthmoving equipment, they worked alongside the TBM crews. "Working with the residents, our volunteers have been able to have a big influence," Henderson said, pointing out people who had "been burned by church in the past" eventually allowed the TBM workers to pray with them and have spiritually meaningful conversations. By mid-October, TBM volunteers cleared sand and gravel from 30 homes, clocked 150 hours of work on heavy machinery and distributed 24 water purifiers.[267] The TBM crews pulled out of Jamestown at the end of October, before the area was covered with ice and snow. However, they resumed cleaning and rebuilding efforts in the summer, working in tandem with BGCT disaster recovery.[268]

Ice storm in North Texas

While the winter meant TBM disaster relief workers had to take a hiatus from their work in Colorado, it did not hinder their work in responding to winter-related storm damage close to home. In mid-December 2013, a devastating ice storm paralyzed much of North Texas, and chainsaw crews went to work clearing broken limbs from rooftops. Assisted by Baptist volunteers from Mississippi and New Mexico, the TBM crews completed about 200 jobs spread out over several counties.[269]

One of those out-of-state volunteers, Wayne Turner from Hatch, N.M., led four people to faith in Christ. While he served with a chainsaw crew working on a home in Garland, a woman who saw the workers asked how much they would charge to cut down a tree in her yard across the street. Turner explained the volunteers would not accept any money for their labor; rather, they just want to help people in Jesus' name. As he and the woman, Esther, talked further, he learned she was divorced, and her daughter and

267. Ken Camp, "TBM volunteers remove obstacles to the gospel in Colorado," Oct. 22, 2013, https://www.baptiststandard.com/news/texas/15691-tbm-volunteers-remove-obstacles-to-the-gospel-in-colorado.

268. "Texas Tidbits: Disaster recovery trips set for summer," April 27, 2014, https://www.baptiststandard.com/news/texas/16390-texas-tidbits-disaster-recovery-trips-set-for-summer.

269. Ken Camp, "Baptist chainsaw crews share faith and clear limbs," Jan. 10, 2014, https://www.baptiststandard.com/news/texas/15974-baptist-chainsaw-crews-share-faith-and-clear-limbs.

granddaughter lived with her. She began to cry as she described her family's troubled situation, and Turner tried to console her. When he turned the conversation to spiritual matters, Esther confided she had no confidence she would spend eternity in heaven. So, Turner shared the gospel with her, and she professed faith in Christ. The next day, the crew worked at Esther's house. While they worked, her daughter returned home and remarked, "Mama sure was different last night." She asked Turner what he had said that made such a difference in her mother. Turner presented the New Testament plan of salvation to her, and the woman also professed Christ. Later, at the Dixon Missions Equipping Center in east Dallas, where the out-of-town crews bunked each night, Turner led to Christ a mother and daughter who worked with the janitorial service that cleaned the building. After the pair accepted Christ as Savior, Turner gave them a Spanish-language Bible, and they asked where they could find a Spanish-language church to attend. "It's wonderful what God can do," Turner said later. "That's why I'm involved in disaster relief. I want to go tell people about Jesus. And in the meantime, if I can do a little chainsaw or mud-out work, that's fine, too."[270]

Ministry in the Pacific Islands

In early November 2013, the Philippines sustained catastrophic damage from one of the most intense tropical cyclones on record, Typhoon Haiyan—known to people in the Philippines as Super Typhoon Yolanda. Estimates varied widely regarding the number of people killed and injured, but it left about 3 million homeless. Bob Young, a TBM volunteer from The Heights Baptist Church in Richardson, and Russell Shieck from First Baptist Church in Ralls, already were planning a trip to the Philippines before the typhoon hit to train pastors in water purification techniques. They delivered 290 water purification units, working closely with Pastor Derick Jacinto from International Baptist Church in Manila. They directed their attention to the Bicol region, at the southern tip of Luzon Island, and to an area in the Eastern Visayas. In addition, TBM shipped 10,000 water filters to the southern Philippines. TBM worked in partnership with Remote Island Ministries, sponsored by Victory Missionary Baptist Church in Sherwood, Ark., which focused primarily on the southernmost part of the island of Mindinao, in the Gulf of Davao region. [271]

An assessment team that included representatives of TBM and the BGCT disaster recovery program journeyed to the province of Iloilo, where the

---

270. *Ibid.*

271. Ken Camp, "Texas Baptists respond to crisis in Philippines," Nov. 27, 2013, https://www.baptiststandard.com/news/texas/15835-texas-baptists-respond-on-multiple-fronts-to-crisis-in-philippines.

typhoon was reported to have destroyed 95 percent of the homes in the coastal towns of Estancia, Carles and Conception. The team worked in conjunction with the Convention of Philippine Baptist Churches. Members of the assessment team included Ernest and Cecile Dagohoy from First Philippine Baptist Church in Missouri City. Since she is a physician licensed

to practice in the Philippines, she held medical clinics and saw more than 100 patients a day in the churches the team visited. The Dagohoys had started contacting friends and family in their homeland the day after the storm hit. So, the Texas team

TBM Disaster Relief volunteer Duane Bechtold demonstrates how to use a water filter at Estancia Baptist Church in the Philippines.

was able to deliver building materials to help 18 churches and to repair 11 pastors' homes damaged by the storm. TBM volunteers Duane Bechtold and Jack Meyer delivered water filtration systems to pastors and trained them in their use. "I went to the Philippines because Jesus compels me to share his love with our neighbors," Meyer said. "Even though the Filipino people are halfway around the world, they are my neighbors. Jesus' love showed in the faces of the Filipino Baptist pastors as they watched our demonstration of the water filters. Their excitement and joy were precious—pure water so easily attainable, literal waters of life."[272]

An East Texas church with close ties to TBM also responded directly to the disaster in the Philippines. Green Acres Baptist Church in Tyler had a longstanding relationship with Word of Hope Church in Manila and its Hope Leadership Institute. The Manila church launched Operation Hope to provide food, medical supplies and temporary shelter to some of the most hard-hit areas in their country, and the congregation set an initial $100,000 goal for

272. Kalie Lowrie, "Texas team delivers supplies, assesses disaster in Philippines," Dec. 18, 2013, https://www.baptiststandard.com/news/texas/15908-texas-team-delivers-supplies-assesses-disaster-in-philippines.

the effort. At Green Acres, Pastor David Dykes challenged his congregation to provide 10 percent of the goal, but he soon discovered he aimed too low. The first Sunday after Dykes issued the challenge, church members contributed $48,000. By the time Green Acres launched its annual offering for worldwide missions, members had contributed $116,000 to Operation Hope.[273]

In the months that followed, the BGCT disaster recovery program focused its attention on rebuilding homes for Filipino pastors. Texas Baptists committed to rebuild at least 15 homes. At the February 2014 BGCT Executive Board meeting, Dagohoy reported the convention had received funds or pledges for seven homes. By the time the board meeting ended, directors and guests pledged to give the funds for the other eight homes.[274]

In November 2014, TBM workers responded to a disaster of an altogether different kind on another Pacific island. At the invitation of the Hawaii Pacific Baptist Convention, a four-woman TBM crisis response team traveled to Hawaii's Big Island to provide compassion care to children and their families in the expected path of a lava flow from the Kilauea volcano. All four volunteers held specialized certification from the National Organization for Victim Assistance or Critical Incident Management. Two members of the team—Tracy Barber from First Baptist Church in Farmersville and Barbara Henderson from First Baptist Church in Sachse—served with a similar crisis response team after a tsunami hit American Samoa. But the situations were quite different, Barber noted. "The children in Samoa and the children in Hawaii were on opposite sides of loss," she said. "In Samoa, they were dealing with what they already had lost—homes and family members. In Hawaii, they were worried about what they were going to lose."[275]

Less than a week before the team arrived, lava from the Kilauea volcano destroyed a home on the outskirts of Pahoa. Residents recognized the lava inevitably would flow somewhere in their general direction, but they had no idea exactly where or when to expect it. "Many families already had packed boxes, getting ready for evacuation," Barber said. "Kids left for school each morning wondering, 'Will I be able to come home after school?'"[276]

273. Camp, "Texas Baptists respond to crisis in Philippines," Nov. 27, 2013.

274. Ken Camp, "BGCT to study annual meeting, promote evangelistic effort," Feb. 26, 2014, https://www.baptiststandard.com/news/texas/16148-bgct-to-study-annual-meeting-promote-evangelistic-effort.

275. Ken Camp, "TBM team offers compassion care to children in lava's path," Dec. 4, 2014, https://www.baptiststandard.com/news/texas/17243-tbm-team-seeks-to-provide-compassion-care-for-children-in-path-of-lava-flow.

276. Ibid.

When they left Texas, the team thought they would make presentations in school classrooms or conduct workshops for teachers to train them how to recognize signs of emotional distress among pupils. But when the lava flow stalled outside Pahoa and looked as if it might change course, school officials cancelled the presentations. So, the TBM team focused attention on Puna Baptist Church and to residents in its surrounding neighborhoods. The Texas volunteers distributed informational packets and teddy bears imprinted with *"Jesus Loves You"* to participants at a weekly community assembly where public safety officers provided updates on the lava flow's progress. When the pastor of Puna Baptist Church, Alan Tamashiro, had to leave the Big Island to attend a family funeral, the TBM crew also ministered in his absence. Among other duties, they represented Puna Baptist Church at an interdenominational pastors' meeting, where they explained how congregations could minister more effectively to children and families in times of crisis. "The Lord had laid on my heart that we needed to minister to the ministers," said Henrietta Gentry, TBM volunteer chaplain coordinator from First Baptist Church in Vidor. She recognized the stress they faced as they tried to provide ministry to others while their own families lived with uncertainty about whether they would lose their homes. "We started the conversation so they could tell their own stories," she said. "Once one starts sharing, the process really starts. They realize they are not alone in what they are feeling and experiencing."[277]

---

277. *Ibid.*

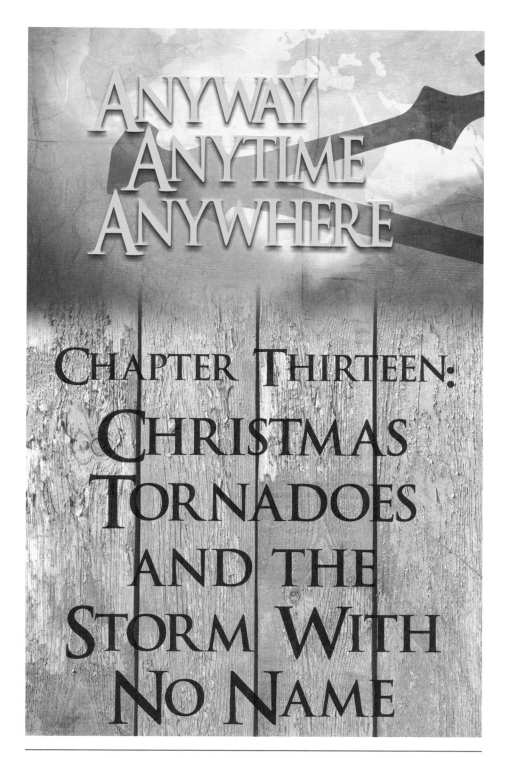

ANYWAY ANYTIME ANYWHERE

CHAPTER THIRTEEN:

CHRISTMAS TORNADOES AND THE STORM WITH NO NAME

CHAPTER THIRTEEN:
CHRISTMAS TORNADOES AND
THE STORM WITH NO NAME

North Texas tornadoes

Bill Blackwell operates a skidsteer to clear property after fires in the Hidden Pines area of Bastrop County.

The measure of disaster relief ministry is not just numbers tabulated. Even so, every number represents a life touched in Jesus' name. In 2015, Texas Baptist Men disaster relief volunteers responded to 35 disasters before Christmas, giving 6,700 volunteer service days. They prepared 44,000 meals, distributed 20,000 boxes to help homeowners collect scattered possessions, provided care for more than 100 children, washed 1,800 loads of laundry and provided access to 2,800 showers. The total for mud-out, ash-out, chainsaw jobs and tarp installations reached 1,300.[278] That included a return to Bastrop County, where wildfires once again swept through the Hidden Pines area. The fires north and west of Smithville spread across more than 4,500 acres, destroying 66 homes, according to the Bastrop County emergency management office. In three weeks, TBM chainsaw crews and other disaster relief volunteers completed 20 job requests from residents.[279]

---

278. Ken Camp, "TBM board hears reports on far-flung ministries," Feb. 24, 2016, https://www.baptiststandard.com/news/texas/18829-tbm-board-hears-reports-on-far-flung-ministries.

279. Ken Camp, "TBM volunteers care for fire and flood survivors," Nov. 5, 2015, https://www.baptiststandard.com/news/texas/tbm-volunteers-care-for-fire-and-flood-survivors/

It had been a busy year, but any thoughts disaster relief volunteers may have entertained about taking a Christmas break vanished the day after Christmas 2015, when a tornado outbreak produced a dozen confirmed tornadoes in eight North and Central Texas counties.[280] An EF 4 tornado that ripped through southeast Garland and Rowlett caused the most intense damage, as a single tornado cut a continuous path of destruction 13 miles long. In all, the tornadoes damaged or destroyed more than 1,400 homes in Ellis, Dallas, Rockwall and Collin counties and caused 13 fatalities— more than half of them in vehicles near the junction of Interstate 30 and the President George Bush Turnpike. First Baptist Church in Rowlett immediately became a ministry center, and its members began collecting diapers, plastic storage containers, gift cards and other items for neighbors in need. The congregation also allowed Texas Baptist

Bill McDowell with the TBM chainsaw crew from Harmony-Pittsburg Baptist Association works in the Hidden Pines area after wildfires swept through Bastrop County.

A TBM chainsaw volunteer from Collin Baptist Association works in a devastated neighborhood in South Garland after tornadoes hit the day after Christmas 2015.

Men to establish its disaster relief incident command center there and set up its mobile command post in front of the church building. A week after the

---

280. National Weather Service, "12/26/15 North TX Tornado Outbreak," https://www. weather.gov/fwd/dec26tornadoes.

tornado hit, TBM had about 80 volunteers representing 17 units at work in the area.[281]

Within 10 days after the tornado unleashed its fury, TBM chainsaw crews completed 100 jobs in the Rowlett and Garland area, and an additional four in Ellis County. In addition, TBM volunteers covered eight homes with blue tarps to keep out rain, provided access to 49 showers, washed 43 loads of laundry and distributed more than 6,600 boxes for residents to reclaim

TBM heavy equipment operators help homeowners in Rowlett clear damaged sites in the aftermath of tornadoes that struck the day after Christmas 2015.

and store scattered possessions. The volunteers also gave away 44 Bibles and dozens of evangelistic gospel tracts. TBM heavy equipment operators worked to remove debris, including a pickup that landed on a home in Garland. Providentially, rather than endangering the residents of the home, it may have saved their lives. When it landed, it bridged two couches in the family's living room, and as the house began to crumble, the resident found shelter from falling debris in the space under the truck.[282]

In Rowlett, TBM disaster relief and the Baptist General Convention of Texas disaster recovery staff worked together, and their time there overlapped considerably more than in most situations. Rowlett city officials asked the BGCT disaster recovery team to organize a volunteer reception center at First Baptist Church to accommodate the significant number of people who wanted to give their time to help remove debris and assist in other ways. In two weekends, 450 volunteers served the area.[283] TBM also worked with

281. Ken Camp, "Texas Baptists respond in wake of North Texas tornadoes," Dec. 29, 2015, https://www.baptiststandard.com/news/texas/18638-texas-baptists-respond-in-wake-of-north-texas-tornadoes.

282. Ken Camp, "TBM volunteers continue to provide disaster relief in North Texas," Jan. 7, 2016, https://www.baptiststandard.com/news/texas/18664-tbm-volunteers-continue-to-provide-disaster-relief-in-north-texas.

283. Leah Reynolds, "Texas Baptists' Disaster Recovery mobilizes 450 volunteers," Jan. 13, 2016, https://www.baptiststandard.com/news/texas/18680-texas-baptists-disaster-recovery-mobilizes-450-volunteers.

church groups who gave 223 volunteer days to work in the area. More than 30 members of South Garland Baptist Church spent a chilly January morning helping a Japanese widow with no insurance and limited English, but TBM provided a retired missionary to Japan who served as interpreter. The tornado had ripped away part of her home's roof, leaving contents in about half the

house rain-soaked and wind-scattered. So, the church group moved her furniture into a temporary storage unit and discarded damaged goods. Then they boxed smaller items and personal possessions, consolidating them in two rooms unaffected by the storm so restoration work could begin on the damaged section of her home.[284]

Wes Sanders, a TBM volunteer from Lake Pointe Church in Rockwall, helps Rowlett residents clear debris after tornadoes swept through the area the day after Christmas 2015.

TBM determined in late January to move from a broad-based, day-to-day presence to specialized teams who could serve on request. In one month, trained TBM disaster relief workers served 1,487 volunteer days in the area, and they coordinated individuals and church groups who contributed 485 volunteer days. By day 31, TBM volunteers had completed 152 chainsaw jobs and 186 debris removal projects, and they covered 30 homes with tarps as temporary roofing. Heavy equipment operators had logged 237 hours. TBM workers provided access to 347 showers, washed 242 loads of laundry, prepared 8,918 meals for volunteers and emergency services personnel, and distributed 5,136 boxes. Volunteer chaplains made 281 contacts. TBM workers distributed 123 Bibles and recorded four professions of faith in Jesus.[285]

284. Ken Camp, "TBM tops 1,000 volunteer days—and still counting—after tornadoes," Jan. 14, 2016, https://www.baptiststandard.com/news/texas/18690-tbm-tops-1-000-volunteer-days-and-still-counting-after-tornadoes.

285. Ken Camp, "TBM shifting gears—not pulling out—after month in Rowlett," Jan. 28, 2016, https://www.baptiststandard.com/news/texas/18740-tbm-shifting-gears-not-pulling-out-after-month-in-rowlett.

Rainy season brings floods to East Texas and Houston

When drenching rain flooded low-lying areas throughout East Texas in March 2016, TBM disaster relief responded. By March 12, trained volunteers in Kilgore began assessing needs, an emergency food-service team was preparing meals, and mud-out crews were shoveling mud from homes, ripping out soaked carpet, removing damaged drywall, and power-washing and disinfecting surfaces to prevent mold and mildew.[286] Near Caddo Lake, Texas-based mud-out teams worked alongside a crew from Utah. In Orange County, a TBM incident

TBM volunteers set up a field kitchen in the back parking lot of the West Conroe Baptist Church campus, where they prepared meals for multiple shelters when floods hit the greater Houston area in late May 2016. On-site coordinator Gary Finley, a layman at West Conroe Baptist, put into practice skills he learned during his career as an air-traffic controller during the busy operation.

management team coordinated work in the Golden Triangle area, where volunteers prepared more than 2,200 meals and distributed more than 5,200 boxes in the first two weeks after the deluge. Mud-out teams and personnel to staff shower and laundry units worked both in Orange County and in Newton County, about 50 miles away.[287]

After about a month, TBM wrapped up its work in the Caddo Lake area, having donated 176 volunteer days, prepared 470 meals, fulfilled 63 work requests, provided access to 78 showers and washed 75 loads of laundry. However, relief efforts continued in Orange and Newton counties, where

---

286. Ken Camp, "TBM volunteers offer disaster relief in East Texas and Louisiana," March 14, 2016, https://www.baptiststandard.com/news/texas/18898-tbm-volunteers-offer-disaster-relief-in-east-texas-and-louisiana.

287. Ken Camp, "TBM disaster relief workers top 700 volunteer days in East Texas," March 30, 2016, https://www.baptiststandard.com/news/texas/18951-tbm-disaster-relief-workers-top-700-volunteer-days-in-east-texas.

four mud-out crews, three shower and laundry units and an emergency food-service team worked. Even though Calvary Baptist Church in the Newton County community of Deweyville sustained serious flood damage, TBM volunteers and church members used the facility as a ministry point, serving about 200 meals a day from the church's parking lot.[288]

In late April, TBM completed its work from the March floods in East Texas, just in time to begin work in the Greater Houston area.

When the rain-swollen Brazos River overflowed its banks in May 2016, flooding parts of the greater Houston area, TBM disaster relief volunteers like Spencer Seyb from West Conroe Baptist Church responded.

Working in five locations in East Texas, TBM volunteers had donated 1,844 volunteer hours. They prepared 11,113 meals, distributed 8,133 boxes, presented 163 Bibles, provided access to 1,114 showers and washed 1,546 loads of laundry. Mud-out crews had cleaned 143 homes, removed damaged flooring and sheetrock from 159 houses, pressure-washed 49 homes and completed 155 mold-remediation jobs.[289]

TBM disaster relief personnel redirected their attention to areas northwest and southwest of Houston, where the rain-swollen Brazos River reached a century-level high and overflowed its banks. One TBM food-service

288. Ken Camp, "Disaster relief completed at Caddo Lake, continues in Southeast Texas," April 12, 2016, https://www.baptiststandard.com/news/texas/18977-disaster-relief-completed-at-caddo-lake-continues-in-southeast-texas.

289. Ken Camp, "Disaster relief begins in Houston; recovery continues in SE Texas," April 27, 2016, https://www.baptiststandard.com/news/texas/19032-disaster-relief-begins-in-houston-recovery-continues-in-se-texas.

crew set up a field kitchen in the parking lot of First Baptist Church in Rosenberg, alongside a shower and laundry unit. The food-service team prepared meals the American Red Cross delivered to five shelters and numerous neighborhoods throughout Fort Bend County and the surrounding area. Police Chief Dallis Warren, who directed the emergency operations center, said damage assessors confirmed 70 homes in Rosenberg sustained damage, and 192 households had to be evacuated. "So many people have been displaced," he said. "Some people are staying with friends or family, but many have no way to prepare meals. It's a huge benefit to know they can count on two hot meals each day. It really helps start the recovery process for them. It lets them know there are caring people willing to do a whole lot to help this community get back on its feet." [290]

In Conroe, TBM volunteers set up a field kitchen in the back parking lot of the West Conroe Baptist Church campus, where they prepared meals for up to 16 shelters. They also filled insulated containers with food, which American Red Cross workers in a dozen emergency response vehicles delivered to affected areas. In all, the parking lot was a beehive of activity, but on-site coordinator Gary Finley kept it running smoothly. Finley, a layman at West Conroe Baptist, put into practice skills he learned during his career as an air-traffic controller. Meanwhile, inside the church building, members led an already-scheduled Vacation Bible School—unaffected by the flurry of activity in the back parking lot.[291] Other volunteers worked with mud-out crews who served flood-damaged areas around Conroe.

By the third week in June, TBM wrapped up emergency-food service work in support of the American Red Cross after preparing more than 96,000 meals for people affected by the Houston-area floods, although TBM volunteers continued to cook for other disaster relief workers. Six mud-out crews who served in Conroe, Rosenberg and Simonton completed 61 jobs, and TBM volunteers distributed about 4,000 boxes to residents.[292]

Nameless devastation in Louisiana

South Louisiana residents have no trouble naming heartache. Names like Allison, Betsy, Camille, Ike, Isaac, Rita and Katrina stir up memories of pain and loss. Louisianans understand the damage hurricanes cause. People across

290. Ken Camp, "TBM offers disaster relief in wake of record flooding along Brazos," June 8, 2016, https://www.baptiststandard.com/news/texas/19156-tbm-offers-disaster-relief-in-wake-of-record-flooding-along-brazos.

291. *Ibid.*

292. "Around the State: DBU students go to Washington; TBM volunteers prepare 96,000 meals," June 22, 2016, https://www.baptiststandard.com/news/around-the-state/19211-around-the-state-dbu-students-go-to-washington-tbm-volunteers-prepare.

the United States open their hearts and their wallets to respond when death and destruction has a name.

The deluge that swamped South Louisiana in summer 2016 lacked any such easy-to-remember handle. Nonetheless, the storm-with-no-name dumped 20 to 30 inches of rain on the region in two deadly August days—more rain than Hurricane Katrina produced in 2005. Floods caused the closure of Interstate 10 and Interstate 12 for several days. Estimates ranged from 50,000 to 75,000 flooded buildings, and the floods claimed 13 lives.[293]

Louisiana Baptists disaster relief volunteers immediately responded. However, because the storm affected such a large area—and because a majority of the Baptist disaster relief workers in the state were affected directly, either by evacuation orders or flood damage to their own homes—TBM was called to help their neighboring state. TBM established an incident command center at First Baptist Church in Jennings, La.

Most homes in the Jennings city limits escaped the worst of the flooding, and Pastor Jeff Cook at First Baptist knew about only one member family seriously affected. So, even before TBM volunteers arrived, his congregation focused on collecting and delivering supplies to isolated rural residents. In the first week after the floods began, church members provided assistance to about 2,500 households in Jefferson Davis and Acadia parishes. "The only way to get to them was by boat. So, we had people who would pirogue out to them, taking supplies into homes," Cook said, referring to a small flat-bottom boat common in the region.[294]

Once TBM disaster relief crews arrived in Jennings, the volunteers set up their mobile command post, field kitchen and shower and laundry unit at First Baptist. Because the flooding covered such a large area, the American Red Cross focused its attention on the most densely populated areas around Baton Rouge and Lafayette, leaving rural areas to TBM. So, the Baptist volunteers prepared and delivered meals directly to affected residents in Jeff Davis and Acadia parishes, using two mobile food-service vehicles the Salvation Army made available. Mud-out crews went to work, accompanied by volunteer chaplains who offered spiritual counsel and comfort. TBM workers also distributed to flood survivors cold bottled water and sturdy plastic storage bins provided by the SBC North American Mission Board. Meanwhile, TBM leaders led training sessions at churches in the flood-affected areas to equip short-term volunteers for disaster relief duty.

---

293. National Weather Service, "August 2016 Record Flooding," http://www.weather.gov/lix/August2016flood.

294. Ken Camp, "TBM offers relief to isolated flood victims in South Louisiana," Aug. 24, 2016, https://www.baptiststandard.com/news/texas/19432-tbm-offers-relief-to-flood-victims-in-isolated-south-louisiana.

One TBM mud-out crew worked on Betty Deshotel's home in Lake Arthur. Like all her neighbors, she was evacuated when the area flooded. When she returned, she discovered her damaged home. In the 30 years she lived in the house, it only flooded one other time, she noted, and the August 2016 flood was worse. However, she found comfort and encouragement in the Christian compassion the TBM volunteers displayed. "I can never pay back" their kindness, she said. "But it makes me want to do something for someone else."[295] By the end of August, mud-out crews had torn out damaged drywall and flooring from about three-dozen homes, provided mold remediation for an equal number and power-washed surfaces in at least nine houses, and the number of requests for their assistance continued to increase. At that point, TBM disaster relief workers had logged more than 500 volunteer days and made more than 450 ministry contacts, prepared about 1,800 meals, distributed more than 2,100 boxes and given away 75 Bibles.[296]

In the days and weeks that followed, other Texas Baptists joined TBM volunteers in ministering to flood survivors in Louisiana. Over Labor Day weekend, 56 Hispanic Texas Baptists from 10 churches and Baptist University of the Américas worked in the Baton Rouge area with Istrouma Baptist Church and Istrouma En Español, while TBM volunteers continued to serve about 100 miles to the west in Jefferson Davis and Arcadia parishes. At the same time, Buckner International provided more than 3,500 items worth about $50,000 to Baton Rouge, including shoes, clothing, blankets and food.[297] Several weeks later, more than 50 student-athletes, coaches and Baptist Student Ministries volunteers from East Texas Baptist University spent their fall break in Baton Rouge working with churches and homeowners to repair flood-damaged buildings.[298]

As other volunteers began helping with the long-term recovery process, TBM wrapped up its disaster relief ministry in Louisiana. Five weeks after the storm deluged South Louisiana, TBM had devoted 1,269 volunteer days to providing disaster relief. Volunteers working out of the command post established at First Baptist in Jennings cooked more than 4,000 meals,

295. *Ibid.*

296. Ken Camp, "Disaster relief expanding after Louisiana floods," Aug. 31, 2016, https://www.baptiststandard.com/news/texas/19454-disaster-relief-expanding-after-louisiana-floods.

297. Ken Camp, "Hispanic Texas Baptists provide labor of love for Louisiana," Sept. 7, 2016, https://www.baptiststandard.com/news/texas/19477-hispanic-texas-baptists-provide-labor-of-love-for-louisiana.

298. "Around the State: UMHB and ETBU students serve; Baylor awards alumni," Oct. 19, 2016, https://www.baptiststandard.com/news/around-the-state/19613-around-the-state-umhb-and-etbu-students-serve-baylor-awards-alumni.

provided access to 633 showers and washed 365 loads of laundry. Mud-out crews completed 100 jobs, and TBM volunteers distributed more than 4,300 boxes. TBM workers made 1,244 ministry contacts while performing other duties, and volunteer chaplains made an additional 871 contacts. They presented the gospel more than 40 times, distributed 173 Bibles and led at least two people to faith in Christ.[299]

Hurricane Matthew

In late September 2016, Tropical Storm Matthew reached hurricane intensity in the eastern Caribbean, reaching Category 5 strength with 160 mph winds as it swept across the coasts of southwestern Haiti, eastern Cuba and western Grand Bahama Island. Later, it hit South Carolina as a Category 1 hurricane, and its effects were felt all along the southeastern coast of the United States. The storm directly caused 585 deaths, with the vast majority occurring in Haiti, making it the deadliest Atlantic hurricane in 11 years.[300]

Texas Baptist missionaries Ernie and Sharon Rice reported western Haiti received the brunt of the wind and rain. The Rices served in Haiti as missionaries jointly appointed by First Baptist Church in Stockdale, South Carolina Baptist Area and the Baptist General Convention of Texas. Ernie Rice—who first traveled to Haiti as a TBM disaster relief volunteer after the earthquakes in 2010—journeyed from Port-au-Prince to western Haiti to assess needs and check on pastors in the region. "Leaves, limbs and whole trees were on the road and in the neighborhoods (east of Leoganne). The banana orchards, sugar cane fields and row crops were flattened and a total loss. Rocks and boulders were on the roads where landslides had occurred," he reported, noting the heaviest damage was caused by rain and flooding. "The highway, in places, had huge piles of soil where runoff from the mountains had washed over the road leaving the dirt." He discovered a bridge on a major route east of Petit Goave washed away, essentially cutting off truck access to the western part of the island. However, he managed to deliver sacks of rice and beans and tanks of propane to the pastors whose churches were providing shelter to displaced people. The pastor of Croix Hillaire met Rice at the washed-out river crossing and hand-carried the supplies across. In his report, Rice pointed to three critical needs—food and the fuel to cook it, cleaning and hygiene supplies, and personal water

299. Ken Camp, "TBM completes disaster relief work in Louisiana," Sept. 21, 2016, https://www.baptiststandard.com/news/texas/19527-tbm-completes-disaster-relief-work-in-louisiana.

300. National Hurricane Center Tropical Cyclone Report, "Hurricane Matthew: 28 September–9 October 2016," http://www.nhc.noaa.gov/data/tcr/AL142016_Matthew.pdf.

filtration devices. Rice had about 500 ceramic water filters from TBM, suitable for a two-bucket drip filtration system, but he needed buckets.[301]

TBM provided personnel and supplies for disaster relief on multiple fronts after Hurricane Matthew. TBM sent a crate to Haiti filled with baby formula and baby-care supplies, along with a solar-operated water pump, to benefit Three Angels Children's relief, a ministry that serves orphans and at-risk Haitian children. A TBM water purification crew and assessment team journeyed to Cuba, where TBM provided two high-capacity water purification units for community use. Since TBM had trained and equipped leaders of the Western Baptist Convention of Cuba for disaster relief, the organization focused primarily on supporting the western convention's ministry to its sister convention in the east. Texas Baptist layman L.M. Dyson worked with multiple organizations, churches and parachurch groups to facilitate the shipment of several containers filled with food, building materials and equipment, including two chainsaws and a generator TBM provided. Meanwhile, TBM sent three chainsaw crews and a skid-steer to First Baptist Church in Palm Coast, Fla., and supplied a mobile shower and laundry unit for military personnel and first-responders in Elizabethtown, N.C. When North Carolina Baptists reported insulated food containers were in short supply, TBM sent a truckload to Whitehall, N.C. A TBM food-service crew and incident management team also provided support for Missouri Baptist disaster relief workers in Whitehall.[302] By the time TBM wrapped up its involvement in disaster relief following Hurricane Matthew, volunteers had donated 688 volunteer days, preparing 14,525 meals, providing access to 333 showers, washing 298 loads of laundry, completing 53 chainsaw jobs, presenting the gospel more than two-dozen times and distributing 46 Bibles. They recorded three professions of faith in Christ.[303]

301. Ken Camp, "Updated: Baptists serve hurricane victims on multiple fronts," Oct. 12, 2016, https://www.baptiststandard.com/news/texas/19597-baptists-serve-hurricane-victims-on-multiple-fronts.

302. Ken Camp, "TBM volunteers continue disaster relief in wake of Hurricane Matthew," Oct. 19, 2016, https://www.baptiststandard.com/news/texas/19621-tbm-volunteers-continue-disaster-relief-in-wake-of-hurricane-matthew.

303. "Around the State: UMHB music students compete; TBM volunteers meet needs along the Rio Grande," Nov. 30, 2016, https://www.baptiststandard.com/news/around-the-state/19769-around-the-state-umhb-music-students-compete-tbm-ministers-along-rio-grande.

ANYWAY ANYTIME ANYWHERE

CHAPTER FOURTEEN:

CHANGING TIMES AND AN UNCHANGING MISSION

CHAPTER FOURTEEN: CHANGING TIMES AND AN UNCHANGING MISSION

Robert Ross (left) and Clyde McMinn from Wylie Baptist Church in Abilene work on repairs and renovations of a home in northwest Houston during the Super Week of Caring in January 2017. The previous fall, TBM assumed responsibility for long-term recovery and rebuilding, assignments previously filled by the Baptist General Convention of Texas.

Texas Baptist Men has a distinguished 50-year history as a pioneering organization. TBM blazed the trail and set the standard for disaster relief ministry among Southern Baptists. It led the way in terms of involving high-school-aged young men in challenging missions activities and mobilizing volunteers in building for the glory of God. It remained open to innovation in areas as varied as restorative justice ministry and providing pure water to people in need. It demonstrated what it looks like when a missions organization seeks to respond to God's invitations rather than program-driven goals.

One of those invitations developed out of conversations with leaders of the Baptist General Convention of Texas regarding disaster recovery. For several years, TBM and the BGCT operated with a mutual understanding—TBM would provide a variety of relief ministries in the immediate aftermath of disasters, and the BGCT would work with local long-term recovery committees and develop church-to-church partnerships to facilitate recovery and rebuilding efforts. While the lines sometimes blurred, personnel directly involved understood the distinction and worked cooperatively. However, many churches and individuals around the state struggled to understand where to contribute and who was responsible for what. Furthermore, as the BGCT Executive Board staff looked at ways to streamline operations— moving from its own four-story building adjacent to the Baylor Health Care System's central campus in Dallas to a shared office building eight miles to the north—it made sense to explore whether TBM should assume responsibility for the continuum of disaster ministries. "It's a natural fit and a logical progression," TBM Executive Director Mickey Lenamon said.[304]

Elmo Johnson, pastor of Rose of Sharon Missionary Baptist Church in Houston's Fourth Ward, works on a TBM-sponsored home-repair project in the Acres Home neighborhood where he grew up.

The executive committee of the TBM executive board agreed, unanimously approving a memorandum of understanding between TBM and the BGCT, saying TBM would accept duties related to disaster recovery, effective Nov. 1, 2016. Under the terms of the agreement, the BGCT said it would help TBM establish an annual offering it will promote in Texas Baptist churches each summer. The BGCT also agreed to give its disaster recovery trailer and van to TBM, adding to its disaster relief fleet of rolling stock. Two BGCT staff members who worked as disaster relief specialists—Marla Bearden and Gerald Davis—became TBM employees for several months, with the BGCT continuing to provide their salary and benefits for a transitional period. The BGCT held onto one disaster-related ministry—its Bounce program that involves students in disaster recovery. The BGCT pledged to give TBM all disaster relief funds it receives, and TBM agreed to provide up to $10,000 per year for Bounce and up to $10,000 annually for rapid-response disaster grants to churches and associations.[305]

---

304. Ken Camp, "Texas Baptist Men responsible for both disaster relief and recovery," Oct. 5, 2016, https://www.baptiststandard.com/news/texas/19555-texas-baptist-men-responsible-for-both-disaster-relief-and-recovery.

305. *Ibid.*

In addition to eliminating confusion and allowing Baptists in Texas to respond to individuals and communities affected by disaster in a coordinated fashion, the transfer of disaster recovery to TBM also fits into a goal Lenamon and his staff recognized as essential to TBM's future—expanding opportunities to involve churches in hands-on ministry. "We need to focus on volunteerism, and we want to work at getting Baptist churches involved with us," Lenamon said soon after his election as executive director. "Texas Baptist Men's purpose is not to take people out of churches but to make them better church members. We are not here to take people out of churches but to make them better church members. We are not here to take the place of the local church but to help take the church and its ministries outside its walls. Being a good volunteer in missions and being a good church member go hand in hand."[306]

The expanded role for TBM in the aftermath of disasters also allows volunteers greater opportunities for direct ministry to survivors, said John-Travis Smith, TBM chief operating officer. "This will give us even more opportunities for hands-on contact with the people we want to help," he said, adding it fits with an overall trend in disaster relief.[307] In past decades, TBM food-service crews prepared tens of thousands of meals the American Red Cross delivered to people in shelters. In recent years, the government increasingly has relied on independent contractors for food preparation. However, while TBM continues to provide meals in times of disaster—often on a somewhat smaller scale than previously—more disaster relief volunteers work in ministries such as mud-out crews after floods, ash-out teams after fires, chainsaw teams, box distribution and volunteer chaplaincy. Long-term disaster recovery provides one additional avenue for direct ministry to people who have lived through disaster.

Long-term recovery also allows volunteers to build relationships with the families with whom they minister. As volunteers provide a continuum of care, they have more opportunities to share the gospel—both through loving actions and through words of Christian witness. "We are able to go deeper with the families," Gerald Davis said. "We come to understand who they are. … It's entering into their lives, walking with them through the journey and going deeper."[308]

306. Ken Camp, "Lenamon elected Texas Baptist Men executive director," May 11, 2016, https://www.baptiststandard.com/news/texas/19074-lenamon-elected-texas-baptist-men-executive-director.

307. Ken Camp, "TBM celebrates 50 years of responding to invitations from God," Jan. 24, 2017, https://www.baptiststandard.com/news/texas/19900-tbm-celebrates-50-years-of-responding-to-invitations-from-god.

308. Ken Camp, "Rebuild homes, restore hope," *Common Call*, Spring 2017, p. 25.

It also presents opportunities for TBM to address another need—involving young adults in ministry. TBM maintains strong Royal Ambassador and Challenger programs for boys and teenaged young men. Retired individuals fill the ranks of trained disaster relief teams and building crews, along with individuals who still are in the workforce but who have accrued enough vacation and seniority to take time away from their jobs without great difficulty. However, one challenge TBM faces as it enters its second 50 years is engaging 20-something, 30-something and 40-something individuals in missions and ministry. Short-term missions projects related to disaster recovery—particularly projects accessible to churches of all sizes—provide good opportunities for involving the younger generation.

Long-term recovery also presents expanded opportunities for an ever-growing segment of TBM life—women. Since the beginning of TBM, women have played important roles. The wives of builders always had an effective ministry wherever building teams have worked, but a growing number of construction crews also include women. Women always have led in emergency child care ministries after disasters. In recent years, however, female representation on food-service crews has increased significantly, and some disaster-related ministries such as box distribution and volunteer chaplaincy particularly have drawn a large number of women. In terms of water ministry, women lead in teaching hygiene and sanitation, as well as distributing water filters and training people to use them.

It's not surprising, then, that TBM has considered emphasizing the "TBM" brand in marketing itself while retaining the "Texas Baptist Men" as the organization's legal name. It not only makes sense in terms of properly representing the group's volunteer base, but also eliminates what some see as provincial—the terms "Texas" and "Baptist." After all, the organization is worldwide in its scope of ministry, and the group long has been willing to partner with likeminded individuals beyond Baptist ranks.

Even so, some would argue Baptists in Texas need Texas Baptist Men to retain its name to enhance their own reputation. At a time when many associate Baptists with controversy or political wrangling, the public at large associates Texas Baptist Men with acts of mercy and kindness. The general public may know or care little about issues that have divided Baptist conventions and congregations, but they know Texas Baptist Men as the group that moves in to help people when disasters strike.

An incident in Southeast Texas illustrates the point. Long-term recovery volunteers with TBM arrived at a home to hang drywall, replace a warped subfloor and repair other damage from flooding. "I remember when y'all were here before," the homeowner said. In fact, none of the volunteers for the home-repair project had met her before. But a TBM disaster relief team had helped her family with mud-out in the immediate aftermath of flooding and provided boxes for the family to collect and store salvageable possessions. However, she remembered the name—"Texas Baptist Men"—and she knew who had helped her family months earlier. "The reputation of Texas Baptist Men is a boost" to long-term recovery, Marla Bearden said. "Wherever we go with TBM, we're recognized."[309]

Terry Henderson stated the matter even more succinctly: "The trust is already there."[310]

Indeed, it is. Texas Baptist Men earned it.

---

309. Camp, "Rebuild Homes, Restore Hope," CommonCall, p. 24.
310. *Ibid.*

Anyway Anytime Anywhere Volume II

APPENDIX

Texas Baptist Men Organization

(Based on information in available TBM directories and board meeting minutes)

State Officers

1999-2000

President — Robert E. (Bob) Dixon, Dallas

Immediate Past President — George E. (Andy) Andreason, McGregor

Recording Secretary — Noe Vella, Corpus Christi

Vice Presidents:

Ag Missions — DeWayne Williams, Arlington

Aviation — John LaNoue Sr., Tyler

Challengers — Larry Blanchard, Lindale

Communications — Mel Goodwin, Kilgore

Couples on Mission — Dick Moody, Ennis

Education — Damon Hollingsworth, Spicewood

Finance — Joe T. Lenamon, Fort Worth

Hispanic Baptist Men — Ambrosio "Butch" Benitez, New Braunfels

Kingdom Renewal — Gene Wofford, Santa Fe

Korean Baptist Men — T.Y. Chung, Farmers Branch

Medical/Dental Fellowship — B.B. Westbrook, Beaumont

Military Fellowship — Jerry Horn, Universal City

Outdoor Fellowship — Bryan Finley, Kerrville

Personnel — Leo Smith, LaMarque

Policy — Jerry Bob Taylor, Brownwood

Restorative Justice Ministry — Mark Hollis, Crowley

Retiree Builders — James Butler, Manor

Retiree Camp Builders — Glen Smith, Sundown

Retiree Special Projects Builders — Jack Tennison, McQueeney

Royal Ambassadors — James Corliss Jr., San Antonio

Veterinarians — Glen Gaines, Brenham

2000-2001

President — Robert E. (Bob) Dixon, Dallas

Recording Secretary —
Noe Vella, Corpus Christi

Vice Presidents:

Ag Missions —
DeWayne Williams, Arlington

Aviation — John LaNoue Sr.,
Tyler

Challengers — Larry Blanchard,
Lindale

Communications — Tom Shelby,
Dallas

Couples on Mission —
Dick Moody, Ennis

Disaster Relief —
Jerry Bob Taylor, Brownwood

Finance — Joe T. Lenamon
Fort Worth

Fire and Rescue —
Mel Goodwin, Kilgore

Hispanic Baptist Men —
Ambrosio "Butch" Benitez,
New Braunfels

Kingdom Renewal —
Gene Wofford, Santa Fe

Korean Baptist Men —
T.Y. Chung, Farmers Branch

Media — Warren Hart, Paris

Medical/Dental —
Robert W. Mann, Arlington

Military Fellowship —
Jerry Horn, Universal City

Outdoor Fellowship —
Bryan Finley, Kerrville

Personnel — Leo Smith,
LaMarque

Policy — George Crews,
Colleyville

Restorative Justice Ministry —
Mark Hollis, Crowley

Retiree Camp Builders —
Hubert Ekstrum, Alvin

Retiree Church Builders —
James Butler, Manor

Retiree Special Projects Builders
— Gene Stapp, Mabank

Royal Ambassadors —
James Corliss Jr., San Antonio

Veterinarian Fellowship —
Glen Gaines, Brenham

Victim Relief Ministries —
Joe Mosley, Dallas

2001-2002

President — Leo Smith, Alvin

Recording Secretary —
Tony Hernandez, San Antonio

Vice Presidents:

Ag Missions —
DeWayne Williams, Arlington

Aviation — John LaNoue Sr.,
Tyler

Brick Layers — Gus Green,
Whitesboro

Cabinet Builders —
Garland Clark, Gary

Camp Builders —
Hubert Ekstrum, Alvin

Church Builders —
Wayne Simpkins, Beeville

Furniture Builders —
Jack Tennison, McQueeney

Special Projects Builders —
James Griffin, Wills Point

Challengers — Larry Blanchard,
Lindale

Communications — Tom Shelby, Dallas

Couples on Mission — Dick Moody, Ennis

Disaster Relief — Jerry Bob Taylor, Brownwood

Finance — Bryan Finley, Kerrville

Fire and Rescue — Mel Goodwin, Kilgore

Hispanic Baptist Men — Ed Alvarado, Donna

Kingdom Renewal — Tommy Malone, McKinney

Korean Baptist Men — Yoo Yoon, Dallas

Media — Warren Hart, Paris

Medical/Dental — Robert W. Mann, Arlington

Military Fellowship — Jerry Horn, Universal City

Outdoor Fellowship — Bryan Finley, Kerrville

Personnel — Kevin Walker, Fort Worth

Policy — George Crews, Colleyville

Restorative Justice Ministry — Mark Hollis, Crowley

Royal Ambassadors — James Corliss Jr., San Antonio

Veterinarian Fellowship — Glen Gaines, Brenham

Victim Relief Ministries — Joe Mosley, Dallas

2002-2003

President — Leo Smith, Alvin

Interim President — Andy Andreason, McGregor

Recording Secretary — Tony Hernandez, San Antonio

Vice Presidents:

Ag Missions — DeWayne Williams, Arlington

Aviation — John LaNoue Sr., Tyler

Brick Layers — Gus Green, Whitesboro

Cabinet Builders — Garland Clark, Gary

Camp Builders — Hubert Ekstrum, Alvin

Church Builders — Wayne Simpkins, Beeville

Furniture Builders — Jack Tennison, McQueeney

Special Projects Builders — James Griffin, Wills Point

Challengers — Larry Blanchard, Lindale

Communications — Tom Shelby, Dallas

Couples on Mission — Dick Moody, Ennis

Disaster Relief — Jerry Bob Taylor, Brownwood

Finance — Bryan Finley, Kerrville

Fire and Rescue — Mel Goodwin, Kilgore

Hispanic Baptist Men — Ed Alvarado, Donna

Kingdom Renewal — Tommy Malone, McKinney

Korean Baptist Men —
Yoo Yoon, Dallas

Media — Warren Hart, Paris

Medical/Dental —
Robert W. Mann, Arlington

Military Fellowship —
Jerry Horn, Universal City

Outdoor Fellowship —
Bryan Finley, Kerrville

Personnel — Kevin Walker, Fort
Worth

Policy — George Crews,
Colleyville

Restorative Justice Ministry —
Mark Hollis, Crowley

Royal Ambassadors —
James Corliss Jr., San Antonio

Veterinarian Fellowship —
Glen Gaines, Brenham

Victim Relief Ministries —
Joe Mosley, Dallas

2003-2004

President — Kevin Walker,
Fort Worth

Recording Secretary —
Tony Hernandez, San Antonio

Vice Presidents:

Ag Missions — Powell Adams,
Lubbock

Aviation — John LaNoue Sr.,
Tyler

Brick Layers — Gus Green,
Whitesboro

Cabinet Builders —
Garland Clark, Gary

Camp Builders —
Ralph Ollman, Burleson

Church Builders —
Wayne Simpkins, Bryan

Furniture Builders —
Jack Tennison, McQueeney

Challengers — Don Roman,
Orange

Communications — Tom Shelby,
Dallas

Couples on Mission —
Fred Johnson, George West

Disaster Relief —
Jerry Bob Taylor, Brownwood

Dixon Building Committee —
Marion "Cotton" Bridges, Plano

Finance — Bryan Finley,
Kerrville

Fire and Rescue —
Mel Goodwin, Kilgore

Hispanic Baptist Men —
Ed Alvarado, Donna

Kingdom Renewal —
Tommy Malone, McKinney

Korean Baptist Men —
Yoo Yoon, Dallas

Media — Bob Mayfield,
Wichita Falls

Medical/Dental —
Robert W. Mann, Arlington

Military Fellowship —
Jerry Horn, Universal City

Outdoor Fellowship —
Bryan Finley, Kerrville

Personnel — Kevin Walker,
Fort Worth

Policy — George Crews,
Colleyville

Restorative Justice Ministry —
Leland Maples, Odessa

Royal Ambassadors —
Butch Durham, LaFeria

Veterinarian Fellowship —
Glen Gaines, Brenham

Victim Relief Ministries —
Joe Mosley, Dallas

2004-2005

President — Tommy Malone,
Dallas

Recording Secretary —
Tony Hernandez, San Antonio

Vice Presidents, Administrative:

Finance — Roger Hall,
Midlothian

Personnel — Randy Newberry,
Round Rock

Policy — Gene Wofford,
Santa Fe

Vice Presidents, Fellowship/
Committee:

Ag Missions — Powell Adams,
Lubbock

Aviation — Tommy Tollett,
Sunrise Beach

Builders

Cabinet Builders —
Sidney Townsend, Sumner

Camp Builders —
Ralph Ollman, Burleson

Church Builders —
Wayne Simpkins, Bryan

Furniture — Jack Tennison,
McQueeney

Masonry — Gus Green,
Whitesboro

Projects — Chuck Cosper,
Hereford

Challengers — Don Roman,
Orange

Church Renewal —
Tommy Malone, McKinney

Communications — Fred Grice,
Corsicana

Couples on Mission —
Fred Johnson, George West

Disaster Relief — Gary Smith,
Addison

Dixon Building —
"Cotton" Bridges, Plano

Hispanic Baptist Men —
Javier Rios, Dallas

Korean Baptist Men —
Peter Lee, Euless

Media — Bob Mayfield, Wichita
Falls

Medical/Dental — Terry Elder,
Corpus Christi

Military — Jerry Horn,
Universal City

Outdoor — Bryan Finley,
Kerrville

Restorative Justice Ministry —
Leland Maples, Odessa

Royal Ambassadors —
Butch Durham, LaFeria

Veterinary — Bill Childers,
Bryan

Victim Relief Ministries —
Harold Sellers, Wharton

2005-2006

President — Tommy Malone,
McKinney

Recording Secretary —
Leo Guerra, Austin

Vice Presidents, Administrative:

Finance — Roger Hall, Midlothian

Personnel — Randy Newberry, Round Rock

Policy — Gene Wofford, Santa Fe

Vice Presidents, Fellowship/Committee:

Ag Missions — Powell Adams, Lubbock

Sunrise Beach Builders

Director — Bill Pigott, Livingston

Cabinet Builders — Sidney Townsend, Sumner

Camp Builders — Ralph Ollman, Burleson

Church Builders — Darwin Watson, Fort Worth

Furniture — Jack Tennison, McQueeney

Masonry — Gus Green, Whitesboro

Projects — Chuck Cosper, Hereford

Challengers — Don Roman, Orange

Church Renewal — Everett Dodson, Spring Branch

Communications — Fred Grice, Corsicana

Couples on Mission — Dick Moody, Ennis

Disaster Relief — Ernie Rice, Stockdale

Dixon Building — Al Wise, Arlington

Hispanic Baptist Men — Javier Rios, Dallas

Korean Baptist Men — Peter Lee, Euless

Media — Steve Darilek, Bridgeport

Medical/Dental — Robert Mann, Arlington

Men's Ministry — Steve Chun, Houston

Military — Jerry Horn, Universal City

Outdoor — Bryan Finley, Kerrville

Restorative Justice Ministry — Leland Maples, Odessa

Royal Ambassadors — Butch Durham, LaFeria

Veterinary — Bill Childers, Bryan

Victim Relief Ministries — Harold Sellers, Wharton

Western Heritage — Shannon Moreland, Commerce

2006-2007

President — Tommy Malone, McKinney

Recording Secretary — Mike Tello, Edcouch

Vice Presidents, Administrative:

Finance — Roger Hall, Midlothian

Personnel — Kevin Walker, Fort Worth

Policy — Jerry Nichols, Forney

Vice Presidents, Fellowship/
Committee:

Ag Missions —
DeWayne Williams, Mansfield

Aviation — Bill Arnold, Dallas

Challengers — Rooster Smith,
Hempstead

Church Renewal —
Everett Dodson, Spring Branch

Communications —
David Jones, McCamey

Couples on Mission —
J.R. Mathews, Hawkins

Dixon Building — Al Wise,
Arlington

Hispanic Baptist Men —
Leo Guerra, Austin

Korean Baptist Men —
Bong Hee Han, Tyler

Media — Steve Darilek,
Bridgeport

Medical/Dental — Robert Mann,
Arlington

Men's Ministry — Red Colquitt,
Cedar Hill

Military — Warren Hart, Paris

Outdoor — Bryan Houser,
Canyon

Restorative Justice Ministry —
Mark Hollis,
North Richland Hills

Royal Ambassadors —
Henry Klingemann, Austin

Veterinary — Bill Childers,
Bryan

Victim Relief Ministries —
Gary Hearon, Dallas

Western Heritage —
Charles Oliver, Waxahachie

2007-2008

President — Tommy Malone,
McKinney

Recording Secretary —
Mike Tello, Edcouch

Vice Presidents, Administrative:

Finance — Roger Hall,
Midlothian

Personnel — Kevin Walker,
Fort Worth

Policy — Jerry Nichols, Forney

Vice Presidents, Fellowship/
Committee:

Ag Missions —
DeWayne Williams, Mansfield

Aviation — Bill Arnold, Dallas

Builders — Bill Campbell,
Athens

Challengers — Rooster Smith,
Hempstead

Church Renewal —
Everett Dodson, Spring Branch

Communications —
David Johnson, Azle

Couples on Mission —
J.R. Mathews, Hawkins

Disaster Relief —
Joe Detterman, McKinney

Dixon Building — Al Wise,
Arlington

Hispanic Baptist Men —
Leo Guerra, Austin

Korean Baptist Men —
Bong Hee Han, Tyler

Media — Steve Darilek,
Bridgeport

Medical/Dental — Robert Mann, Arlington

Men's Ministry — Red Colquitt, Cedar Hill

Military — Warren Hart, Paris

Outdoor — Bryan Finley, Kerrville

Restorative Justice Ministry — Mark Hollis,
North Richland Hills

Royal Ambassadors — Rooster Smith, Hempstead

Veterinary — Bill Childers, Bryan

Victim Relief Ministries — Gary Hearon, Dallas

Western Heritage — Charles Oliver, Waxahachie

2008-2009

President — Al Wise, Arlington

Recording Secretary — Mike Tello, Elsa

Vice Presidents, Administrative:

Finance — Bryan Finley, Kerrville

Personnel — Kevin Walker, Fort Worth

Policy — Jerry Nichols, Forney

Vice Presidents, Fellowship/Committee:

Ag Missions — DeWayne Williams, Mansfield

Aviation — Bill Arnold, Dallas

Builders — Bill Campbell, Athens

Church Renewal — Tommy Malone, McKinney

Communications — Danny Shaver, Gainesville

Couples on Mission — J.R. Mathews, Hawkins

Disaster Relief — Joe Detterman, McKinney

Dixon Building — Edd Waltrip, Plano

Hispanic Baptist Men — Leo Guerra, Austin

Korean Baptist Men — Bong Hee Han, Tyler

Media — Bob Mayfield, Wichita Falls

Medical/Dental — Jerry Pentacost, Point Comfort

Men's Ministry — Jerry Smith, Hurst

Military — David Dinkins, LaMarque

Outdoor — Bryan Houser, Canyon

Restorative Justice Ministry — Mark Hollis,
North Richland Hills

Royal Ambassadors — Henry Klingemann, Austin

Special Needs — Elgin Taylor, Houston; and Mike Bradley, Powderly

Veterinary — Bob Denton, Grandview

Victim Relief Ministries — Clifford Harden, San Antonio

Water Ministry — Bob Young, Fairview

Western Heritage — Charles Oliver, Waxahachie

2009-2010

President — Al Wise, Arlington

Recording Secretary —
Mike Tello, Elsa

Vice Presidents, Administrative:

Finance — Bryan Finley,
Kerrville

Personnel — Bill Noble,
Lubbock

Policy — Jerry Nichols, Forney

Vice Presidents, Fellowship/
Committee:

Ag Missions —
DeWayne Williams, Mansfield

Aviation — Bill Arnold, Dallas

Builders — Bill Campbell,
Athens

Challengers — John Travis
Smith, Hempstead

Church Renewal —
Tommy Malone, McKinney

Communications — Ron Parker,
Lake Jackson

Couples on Mission —
Matt Patterson, Plano

Disaster Relief — Ernie Rice,
Stockdale

Dixon Building — Edd Waltrip,
Plano

Hispanic Baptist Men —
Leo Guerra, Austin

Korean Baptist Men —
Bong Hee Han, Tyler

Media — Bob Mayfield,
Wichita Falls

Medical/Dental —
Jerry Pentacost, Point Comfort

Men's Ministry —
Mark Clemons, Kerrville

Military — Bob Presley, Boerne

Outdoor — Bryan Houser,
Canyon

Restorative Justice Ministry —
Roger Hollar, Fort Worth

Royal Ambassadors —
Murrie Wainscott, Italy

Veterinary — Bob Denton,
Grandview

Victim Relief Ministries —
Clifford Harden, San Antonio

Water Ministry — Bob Young,
Fairview

Western Heritage —
Charles Oliver, Waxahachie

2010-2011

President — Al Wise, Arlington

Recording Secretary —
Leo Guerra, Austin

Vice Presidents, Administrative:

Finance — Bryan Finley,
Kerrville

Personnel — Bill Noble,
Lubbock

Policy — Gene Wofford,
Santa Fe

Vice Presidents, Fellowship/
Committee:

Ag Missions — Roy Stanford,
Orange

Aviation — Mike Harwood,
Corsicana

Builders — Bill Campbell,
Athens

Challengers — John Travis
Smith, Hempstead

Church Renewal —
Tommy Malone, McKinney

Communications — Ron Parker,
Lake Jackson

Couples on Mission —
Matt Patterson, Plano

Disaster Relief — Gary Smith,
Addison

Dixon Building — Edd Waltrip,
Plano

Hispanic Baptist Men —
Mike Tello, Elsa

Korean Baptist Men —
DeWayne Williams, Mansfield

Media — Bob Mayfield,
Wichita Falls

Medical/Dental —
Jerry Pentacost, Point Comfort

Men's Ministry —
Mark Clemons, Kerrville

Military — Bob Presley, Boerne

Outdoor — Bryan Houser,
Canyon

Restorative Justice Ministry —
Roger Hollar, Fort Worth

Royal Ambassadors —
Murrie Wainscott, Italy

Veterinary — Bob Denton,
Grandview

Victim Relief Ministries —
Ed Smith, Grand Prairie

Water Ministry — Bob Young,
Fairview

Western Heritage —
Charles Oliver, Waxahachie

2011-2012

President — Tommy Malone,
McKinney

Recording Secretary —
Leo Guerra, Austin

Vice Presidents, Administrative:

Finance — Roger Hall,
Midlothian

Personnel — Bill Noble,
Lubbock

Policy — Gene Wofford,
Santa Fe

Vice Presidents, Fellowship/
Committee:

Ag Missions — Roy Stanford,
Orange

Aviation — Mike Harwood,
Corsicana

Builders — Ed Sandlin, Corinth

Challengers — John Travis
Smith, Hempstead

Church Renewal —
Wayland Peterson, Early

Communications — Ron Parker,
Lake Jackson

Couples on Mission —
Matt Patterson, Plano

Disaster Relief — Gary Smith,
Addison

Dixon Building — Edd Waltrip,
Plano

Hispanic Baptist Men —
Mike Tello, Elsa

Korean Baptist Men —
Bong Hee Han, Tyler

Media — Ronnie Yeatts, Corinth

Medical/Dental — Lee Baggett,
Amarillo

Men's Ministry —
Mark Clemons, Kerrville

Military — Bob Presley, Boerne

Outdoor — Lee Bevly, Utopia

Restorative Justice Ministry — David Valentine, Huntsville

Royal Ambassadors — Murrie Wainscott, Italy

Veterinary — Bob Denton, Grandview

Victim Relief Ministries — Ed Smith, Grand Prairie

Water Ministry — Bob Young, Fairview

Western Heritage — Mike McKinney, Terrell

2012-2013

President — Tommy Malone, McKinney

Recording Secretary — Leo Guerra, Austin

Vice Presidents, Administrative:

Finance — Roger Hall, Midlothian

Personnel — Kevin Walker, Fort Worth

Policy — Gene Wofford, Santa Fe

Vice Presidents, Fellowship/ Committee:

Ag Missions — Roy Stanford, Orange

Aviation — Bill Arnold, Dallas

Builders — Ed Sandlin, Corinth

Challengers — Mike Wade, Waxahachie

Church Renewal — Wayland Peterson, Early

Communications — Mark Boucher, Euless

Couples on Mission — Nolan Presley, Fairview

Disaster Relief — Gary Smith, Addison

Dixon Building — Edd Waltrip, Plano

Hispanic Baptist Men — Mike Tello, Elsa

Korean Baptist Men — Bong Hee Han, Tyler

Media — Ronnie Yeatts, Corinth

Medical/Dental — Lee Baggett, Amarillo

Men's Ministry — Chris Moore, Purdon

Outdoor — Lee Bevly, Utopia

Restorative Justice Ministry — David Valentine, Huntsville

Royal Ambassadors — Steve Darilek, Bridgeport

Veterinary — Bob Denton, Grandview

Victim Relief Ministries — Ed Smith, Grand Prairie

Water Ministry — Bob Young, Fairview

Western Heritage — Mike McKinney, Terrell

2013-2014

President — Kevin Walker, Fort Worth

Recording Secretary — Lane Grayson, Ennis

Vice Presidents, Administrative:

Finance — John Travis Smith, Hempstead

Personnel — Everett Dodson, Spring Branch

Policy — Gene Wofford,
Santa Fe

Vice Presidents, Fellowship/
Committee:

Ag Missions — Eddie Bearden,
Allen

Aviation — Bill Arnold, Dallas

Builders — Jerry Nickerson,
Emory

Challengers — Mike Wade,
Waxahachie

Church Renewal —
Jerry Nichols, Forney

Communications —
Mark Boucher, Euless

Couples on Mission —
Russell Schieck, Floydada

Disaster Relief — Ralph Rogers,
Amarillo

Hispanic Baptist Men —
Ray Carrillo, Tyler

Korean Baptist Men —
Bong Hee Han, Tyler

Media — Bob Mayfield,
Wichita Falls

Medical/Dental — Lee Baggett,
Amarillo

Men's Ministry — Chris Moore,
Purdon

Outdoor — Bryan Finley,
Kerrville

Restorative Justice Ministry —
Tommy Malone, McKinney

Royal Ambassadors —
Steve Darilek, Bridgeport

Veterinary — Bob Denton,
Grandview

Victim Relief Ministries —
Glen Cato, Grand Prairie

Water Ministry — Bob Young,
Fairview

Western Heritage — Lee Bevly,
Utopia

2014-2015

President — Kevin Walker,
Fort Worth

Recording Secretary —
Lane Grayson, Ennis

Vice Presidents, Administrative:

Finance — John Travis Smith,
Hempstead

Personnel — Everett Dodson,
Spring Branch

Policy — Gene Wofford,
Santa Fe

Vice Presidents, Fellowship/
Committee:

Ag Missions — Eddie Bearden,
Allen

Aviation — Bill Arnold, Dallas

Builders — Jerry Nickerson,
Emory

Challengers — Mike Wade,
Waxahachie

Church Renewal —
Jerry Nichols, Forney

Communications —
Mark Boucher, Euless

Couples on Mission —
Russell Schieck, Floydada

Disaster Relief — Ralph Rogers,
Amarillo

Hispanic Baptist Men —
Ray Carrillo, Tyler

Korean Baptist Men —
Bong Hee Han, Tyler

Media — Bob Mayfield,
Wichita Falls

Medical/Dental — Lee Baggett,
Amarillo

Men's Ministry — Chris Moore,
Purdon

Outdoor — Bryan Finley,
Kerrville

Restorative Justice Ministry —
Tommy Malone, McKinney

Royal Ambassadors —
Steve Darilek, Bridgeport

Veterinary — Bob Denton,
Grandview

Victim Relief Ministries —
Glen Cato, Grand Prairie

Water Ministry — Bob Young,
Fairview

Western Heritage — Lee Bevly,
Utopia

2015-2016

President — Kevin Walker,
Fort Worth

Recording Secretary —
Juan Alvarado, Donna

Vice Presidents, Administrative:

Finance — John Clayton,
Houston

Personnel — Bryan Finley,
Kerrville

Policy — Gene Wofford,
Santa Fe

Vice Presidents, Fellowship/
Committee:

Ag Missions — Bob Denton,
Grandview

Aviation — John LaNoue, Frost

Builders — Larry Harrison,
Odessa

Challengers — Bryan Davis,
Belton

Church Renewal — Jerry Nichols,
Forney

Communications —
John Thielepape, Weatherford

Couples on Mission —
Russell Schieck, Floydada

Disaster Relief — Ralph Rogers,
Amarillo

Hispanic Baptist Men —
Tony Garcia, Bay City

Korean Baptist Men —
Benjamin Kim, San Antonio

Media — Steve Darilek,
Bridgeport

Medical/Dental — Lee Baggett,
Amarillo

Men's Ministry — Will Withers,
Buna

Military — Butch Durham,
La Feria

Outdoor — Bryan Houser,
Amarillo

Restorative Justice Ministry —
Tommy Malone, McKinney

Royal Ambassadors —
Murrie Wainscott, Italy

Veterinary — Bob Denton,
Grandview

Victim Relief Ministries —
Win Brown, Plano

Water Ministry — Bob Young,
Fairview; and Dee Dee Wint,
Flower Mound

Western Heritage —
Fred Johnson, George West

2016-2017

President — Gary Smith,
McKinney

Recording Secretary —
Juan Alvarado, Donna

Vice Presidents, Administrative:

Finance — John Clayton,
Houston

Personnel — Bryan Finley,
Kerrville

Policy — Gene Wofford,
Santa Fe

Vice Presidents, Fellowship/
Committee:

Ag Missions — Bob Denton,
Grandview

Aviation — John LaNoue, Frost

Builders — Larry Harrison,
Odessa

Challengers — Bryan Davis,
Belton

Church Renewal —
Jerry Nichols, Forney

Communications —
John Thielepape, Weatherford

Couples on Mission —
Russell Schieck, Floydada

Disaster Relief — Ralph Rogers,
Amarillo

Hispanic Baptist Men —
Tony Garcia, Bay City

Korean Baptist Men —
Benjamin Kim, San Antonio

Media — Steve Darilek,
Bridgeport

Medical/Dental — Lee Baggett,
Amarillo

Men's Ministry — Will Withers,
Buna

Military — Butch Durham,
La Feria

Outdoor — Bryan Houser,
Amarillo

Restorative Justice Ministry —
Tommy Malone, McKinney

Royal Ambassadors —
Murrie Wainscott, Italy

Veterinary — Bob Denton,
Grandview

Victim Relief Ministries —
Win Brown, Plano

Water Ministry — Bob Young,
Fairview; and Dee Dee Wint,
Flower Mound

Western Heritage —
Fred Johnson, George West

Staff

2000-2016

Executive Director
Jim Furgerson
Leo Smith
Don Gibson
Mickey Lenamon

Associate Executive Director
Don Gibson
Mickey Lenamon

Chief Operating Officer
John Travis Smith

Adult Mission and Men's
Ministry
John Bullock
Don Gibson

Men's Ministry/Church Renewal

Don Gibson
Randy Newberry

Children and Youth Mission and Ministry Director

Keith Mack

Disaster Relief Director

Dick Talley
Terry Henderson

Donor Relations Associate

Roy Stanford

Ethnic Consultant

Ed Alvarado

Logistics Coordinator

Dick Talley

Facilities/Warehouse Manager

Dick Jenkins
Ron Chapman

Accounting

Gerri Jenkins
Becky Majors
Rhonda Walden
Pam Woodberry

Ministry Assistants

Tracie Bjorkgren
Janice Clary
Alicia Enriquez
Cindy Finn
Jessica Fletcher
Frances Jenkins
Rae Jones
Cathy Lawrence
Pat Luttrell
Jan Newberry
Jeanette Nichols
Linda Woods
Karen Young

About the author

Kenneth Roy Camp has reported on Texas Baptist Men for more than three decades. He served in the communications office of the Baptist General Convention of Texas more than 19 years, including several years as news and information director. Since January 2004, he has been managing editor of the *Baptist Standard*.

He grew up in Greenville, Texas, and graduated from East Texas State University in Commerce and Southwestern Baptist Theological Seminary in Fort Worth. He and his wife, Diane, are members of South Garland Baptist Church in northeastern Dallas County. They have three grown sons with whom they are well pleased, Daniel, Matthew and Nathan; two lovely daughters-in-law, Lindsey and Devon; and a pair of absolutely adorable grandsons, Henry and Andrew.

ANYWAY ANYTIME ANYWHERE
VOLUME II

INDEX

A

Afghanistan, 45

Alabama, 84, 85, 86

Alto Frio Baptist Encampment, 37

Alvarado, Ed, 97, 170, 171, 182

Australia, 16, 44

B

Baptist Child and Family Services (BCFS, CERI), 31, 87, 104, 106

Baptist General Convention of Texas (BGCT), 3, 4, 8, 9, 10, 11, 12, 13, 14, 21, 22, 24, 35, 43, 47, 56, 61, 62, 96, 97,114, 118, 121, 123, 135, 141, 142, 144, 151, 158,163, 164, 182

Barber, Tracy, 144

Barzani, Mafa, 49

Bearden, Marla, 164, 167

Bechtold, Duane, 143

Belize, 23, 44, 76

Blackaby, Henry, 11, 15, 43, 48

Blanchard, Brad, 27

Blanchard, Larry, 109,168-170

Brittain, Mike, 82

Buckner International, 7, 51, 52, 55, 86, 107, 157

(Buckner Benevolences, Buckner Children & Family Services, Buckner Family Pathways) 33

Burks, Larry, 90

Burma, 104

Byrd, Monte, 33

C

Caison, Mickey,74

Campbell, Harry, 61, 72

Campbell, Rex, 62, 121

Canada, 44, 128

Cepeda, Robert, 96

Chandler, Ross, 98

Cheatham, Harold, 37

Children at Heart Ministries (Texas Baptist Children's Home, Gracewood), 83

Colorado, 76-77, 127,133, 139-141

Columbia (Space Shuttle), 81

Cooperative Program, 9, 11, 13-14

Crowder, John, 133

Cuba, 51-55, 106-107, 128, 158-159

Cundiff, James, 116

D

Darilek, Steve, 27, 173-174, 178-181

Davenport, Phil, 67

Davis, Gerald, 164-165

Detterman, Joe, 95, 174-175

Dilday, Russell H., 9

Dixon, Robert E. (Bob), 7, 8, 14, 16, 21, 25, 43, 50, 71, 86, 168

Dyson, L.M., 52, 159

E

El Salvador, 56, 72-73

Esters, Eugene, 36-37

F

Felkner, George, 45

Finley, Garry, 153, 155

Florida, 85-86, 127

Fonseca, Eddie, 72

Furgerson, Jim,4, 8, 31, 181

G

Galindo, Manuel, 52

Gentry, Henrietta, 145

O

Oklahoma, 61, 75, 77, 94-95, 109, 114, 126-127, 135, 138-139

P

Palmer, Jim and/or Viola
Patterson, Harold, 66
Philippines, 1, 113-115, 142-144
Pigott, Bill, 4, 7, 31, 38-39, 173
Posey, Mary Kay and/or Fred, 67
Prewitt, Carroll, 88

R

Rice, Ernie and/or Sharon, 115-117, 158, 173, 176
Riverbend Retreat Center, 31
Rodriguez, Leticia, 56-57
Rouse, Debbie, 50
Royal Ambassadors, 3, 8, 12, 16, 21-24, 44, 53, 88, 133, 168-181

S

Seanor, Zachariah, 26
Sellers, Jered, 72, 77
Shahan, Richard, 125
Shieck, Russell, 142
Shores, Dexton, 97
Smith, Gary, 4, 50-51, 72, 81, 97, 106, 121-122, 127, 172, 177-178, 181
Smith, Jerry, 64, 175
Smith, John-Travis, 16, 165
Smith, Leo, 4, 11-13, 21, 25, 31, 88, 113, 116, 168-170
Smith, Nancy, 135-136
Smith, "Wimpy", 8
Sorrells, Fred, 117
South Africa, 44, 61, 64
South Texas Children's Home, 8, 107
Southern Baptist Convention (SBC), 114, 121, 127
Southern Baptists of Texas Convention (SBTC), 8-13
Sri Lanka, 86-89
Sushi, Hashim, 49

T

Talley, Dick, 4, 61, 87, 114, 117, 123, 125, 182
Tello, Mike, 35, 54, 173-178
Tennison, Jack, 36-37, 168-173
Texas Baptist Encampment at Palacios, 31
Texas Baptist Missions Foundation, 14, 16, 53
Texas Department of Criminal Justice (TDCJ), 47
Thailand, 86, 104-105
Thomas, Robert, 77
Tropical Storm Allison, 73
Typhoon Haiyan, 142

U

Ukraine, 44

V

Valentine, David, 47, 178
Valerio, Josué, 97
Vawter, Larry, 115
Venezuela, 67
Victim Relief Ministries, 46, 75, 81, -82, 86, 94, 96, 128, 169-181
Villanueva, Rey, 94

W

Wainscott, Murrie, 26, 176-180
Wall, Billy Joe, 68
Waller, Terry, 65
Weaver, Herb, 22-24
Wilson, Mike, 37
Wingard, Ron
Wint, Dee Dee and/or Tim, 67, 180-181
Wisdom-Martin, Sandy, 65
Woman's Missionary Union (WMU), 12, 24-26, 53, 65, 66
Wynne Unit, 47-48

Y

Young, Bob, 64-65, 142,175-181

Z

Zimbabwe, 64